The Highlands

m Edinburgh to Inverness

by
F. R. BANKS

Letts Motor Tour Guides

Printed and Published by
Charles Letts & Company Limited
London, Edinburgh & New York

Head Office:
Diary House, Borough Road, London, S.E.1

Publishing Consultant : Lionel Leventhal

Cover Artist : Kenneth Farnhill

Maps : Jack Parker

The Highlands
by F. R. Banks
first published 1969
© Charles Letts & Company Limited, 1969

How to use your
Letts Motor Tour Guide

The best way to see Britain is, for most people, by car. This Tour Guide has been specially designed to lead you—the motorist—to all that is best in its chosen area.

The Highlands from Edinburgh to Inverness

This series of tours covers the whole of the Central Highlands of Scotland, extending north from Edinburgh and Glasgow, and bordered by the Great Glen which runs across country between Fort William and Inverness. This is a region which contains some of the grandest and most beautiful scenery in Britain — delightful inland lochs and deep inlets of the sea, rugged coasts, rich and verdant glens, and imposing mountains, interesting old towns, charming villages, and fascinating castles and other medieval remains.

The Tours

There are ten motor tours in this Guide and each tour covers about 150 miles. If you wish to visit and explore all the places mentioned, you may find that a single tour will provide two or more good days' motoring. All the tours are circular, and so you can start and finish a route at any other point you may choose. This book is yours to use in your own way.

The tours take in all the better-known places of interest in the Central Highlands. They also include many places less well known to the average tourist, though the necessity of covering the whole area within a reasonable mileage has meant the exclusion of some out-of-the-way places.

The mountainous nature of the Highlands and the consequent paucity of roads in this region makes it inevitable that parts of the tours follow main roads, though it must be said that these are by no means congested (especially when compared with those of England), except in certain popular tourist areas, such as The Trossachs and Loch Lomond-side, during the height of summer.

The Maps

The maps (one for each tour and a larger one for the whole area) have been specially designed to show clearly all the information you will need—without being unduly technical. Readers who lack expertise in map-reading will have no difficulty in following the directions and the route. The main approach roads to the tours are also indicated. *continued*

Reference Books

For those who wish to use more detailed maps, Sheets 6 and 7 of the Ordnance Survey quarter-inch maps cover the southern part of the area, including Edinburgh and Glasgow, while Sheets 4 and 5 cover the northern part.

Particulars are given in the tours of the days and times of opening for houses, castles and museums, and these are correct at the time of going to press. The most recent information can be obtained from *Historic Houses, Castles and Gardens in Great Britain,* which is published annually in February. Details regarding museums and art galleries are given in *Museums and Galleries in Great Britain,* published yearly in July.

Particulars of hotels, restaurants and inns are given in the annual reference guide, *Hotels and Restaurants in Britain,* published by the British Travel Association. An annual selective and critical guide to eating places is Raymond Postgate's *Good Food Guide,* and a more extensive annual critical guide to hotels, restaurants, pubs and inns is written by Egon Ronay. All the above books may be purchased from any bookseller, or referred to at a library.

Contents

Maps

Tour Maps are on the first or second page of each tour

N

Kyle of Lochalsh

A87

Invergarry

A82

A86

Mallaig

A830

Spean Bridge

Fort William (9)

A82

Glencoe

A82

A

Killin

A85

Oban (7)(8)

A816

A819

Dalmally

Crianlari

A8

Callar

Inveraray

A83

Arrochar

A821

A83

A814

Aberf

Lochgilphead

A82

Dumb

A8

A83

Greenock

A8

Tarbert

Glasg (4)(5

A78

The area covered by this Tour Guide.

Commencing points for tours and tour numbers—
Edinburgh(1)

Elgin

A96

ess

9

Grantown-on-Spey

A95

A939

Aviemore

ngussie

Braemar

A93

Balmoral Castle

A93 Aberdeen

A92

Montrose

A924

A94

chry

A9

Aberfeldy

A926

26

A923

Blairgowrie

Dunkeld

A923

A93

Dundee

A822

A85

A92

Perth

St. Andrews

A9

A90

A91

A918

eff

A915

2

A91

Kinross

A9

A907

A90

A905

Dunfermline

9

Queensferry

A90

A1

A9

Edinburgh

Falkirk

Linlithgow

(1)(2)(3)

Haddington

A8

73

A701

A7

A68

A74

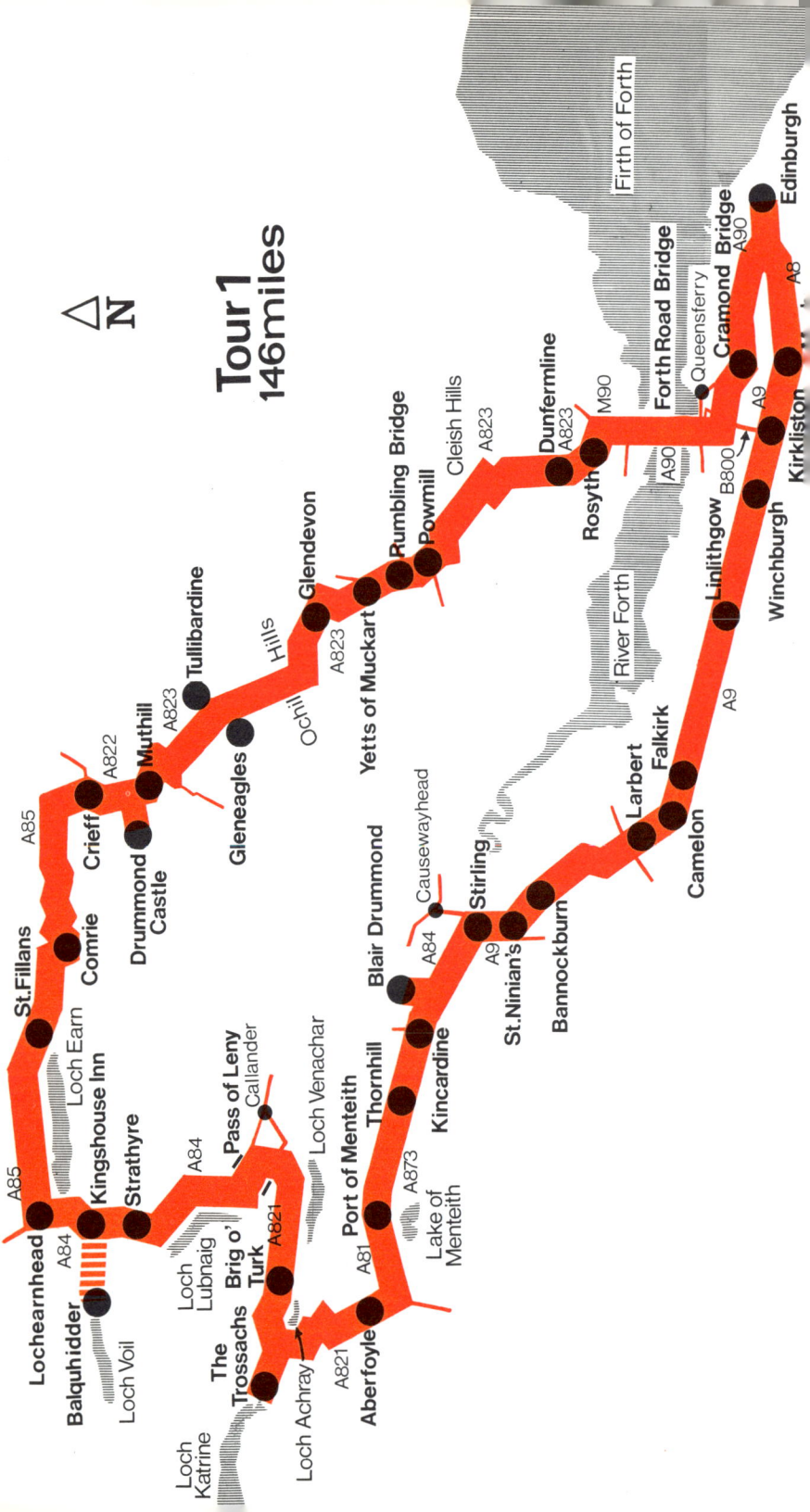

N

Tour 1
146 miles

Firth of Forth

Edinburgh
A8
Cramond Bridge
A90
Queensferry
Forth Road Bridge
Kirkliston
A9
Winchburgh
B800
A90
Linlithgow
A9
M90
Dunfermline
A823
Rosyth
A823
Rumbling Bridge
Powmill
Cleish Hills
A823
Glendevon
Hills
A823
Ochil
Tullibardine
A823
Muthill
A822
Crieff
A85
Gleneagles
Drummond Castle
Yetts of Muckart
Comrie
St.Fillans
Loch Earn
Balquhidder
Lochearnhead
A84
Loch Voil
A85
Kingshouse Inn
Strathyre
A84
Callander
Pass of Leny
Loch Lubnaig
Brig o' Turk
A821
The Trossachs
Loch Achray
Loch Venachar
Loch Katrine
A821
Aberfoyle
A81
Port of Menteith
Lake of Menteith
A873
Thornhill
Kincardine
Blair Drummond
A84
Causewayhead
Stirling
A9
St.Ninian's
Bannockburn
River Forth
Larbert
Falkirk
Camelon
A9

1. Stirling, The Trossachs and Strathearn

The first three tours in this book all start at Edinburgh and they cover the south-east part of the Central Highlands of Scotland, as well as the many places of interest lying between the capital and the Highland frontiers. This tour includes Linlithgow, long famous for its royal palace, and Stirling, equally famous for its royal castle, at the head of a long craggy ridge up which the interesting old town climbs, rather in the manner of the old town and castle of Edinburgh. It also takes in such places of diverse interest as the glorious Field of Bannockburn, a monument to Scottish tenacity and valour, Balquhidder, famous for its associations with Rob Roy, and the well-known golfing resort of Gleneagles. The scenery is perhaps at its finest in the neighbourhood of The Trossachs and the chain of lakes stretching from Loch Venachar by Loch Achray to Loch Katrine, but other beautiful lakes are Loch Lubnaig and Loch Earn, from which the delightful vale of Strathearn extends past Comrie to the favourite tourist centre of Crieff.

From Edinburgh (Princes Street) by A8 via Corstorphine to Maybury (5½ miles), then by A9, passing Edinburgh (Turnhouse) Airport, to Kirkliston (3½ miles).

Kirkliston is a village on a hill, with a large fruit farm and a partly 18th century church incorporating an excellent Romanesque doorway.

A9 on, skirting the oil-shale country, to Winchburgh (2½ miles) and thence to Linlithgow (5½ miles).

Linlithgow, a county town and an old royal burgh, was a place of importance from early medieval times. It has a long High Street, with 16th century and later houses, and numerous fountains. A 16th century gateway admits to the palace precincts, in which is the 15th-16th century St. Michael's Church, one of the finest parish churches in Scotland, with graceful window tracery. The Palace (admission 10 to 7; October-March, 10 to 4; Sundays from 2), a splendid example of a fortified residence, though in ruins, was long a favourite retreat of the Stewart kings, and Mary, Queen of Scots, was born here in 1542. The palace was burned in 1424; the west part of the quadrangle was rebuilt for James I, but the south and east sides, architecturally the finest, were added for James V, who had been born here in 1512. The chief apartments include the Great Hall, with a huge fireplace, the most impressive in Scotland. The palace was accidentally burned again by the Duke of Cumberland's troops, who were quartered here in 1746, during the Jacobite rising.

A9 on for 5½ miles, where A905 branches to the right, and thence for two miles skirting a stretch of the Antonine Wall, to Falkirk. (A905, which avoids the narrow streets of Falkirk, is a dull road and misses the memorials of the Battle of Bannockburn.)

Falkirk, an old market town which has congested streets, is also an old-established manufacturing centre, with famous ironworks and other industries. Beside the Edinburgh road, bordering the public grounds of Callendar Park, is a well-preserved length of the Antonine Wall, a Roman fortification consisting of a turf rampart with a parallel ditch on the north side, constructed in A.D. 138-142 and crossing the neck of Scotland from Old Kilpatrick, on the Clyde, to Bo'ness, on the Forth. The wall was strengthened by some 19 forts (of which few traces remain), but the whole work was abandoned before the end of the 2nd century.

A9 on to Camelon ($1\frac{1}{2}$ miles), and then right, leaving the Glasgow road, to Larbert ($1\frac{1}{2}$ miles). Beyond Larbert the road leaves the industrial belt and affords good views of the Campsie Fells to the west, the Ochil Hills to the north-east, and Stirling Castle and the Wallace Monument ahead, with the frontiers of the Highlands beyond. A9 on to Bannockburn (6 miles) and thence to St. Ninians ($1\frac{1}{2}$ miles).

Bannockburn. The Battle of Bannockburn (1314), in which the Scots, under the redoubtable Robert Bruce, defeated the numerically superior army of Edward II, and secured the independence of Scotland, was fought on the then marshy levels of the Forth to the north of Bannockburn and east of St. Ninians (neither of which then existed). Beside the Glasgow road (Tour 5), $\frac{1}{2}$-mile south of the road junction is a fine Information Centre (1967) of the National Trust for Scotland, and behind this, on the Borestone Brae, where the Scottish king is believed to have raised his standard, are a memorial Rotunda (1964) and a fine equestrian statue of the king, by C. d'O. P. Jackson.

A9 on to Stirling ($1\frac{1}{2}$ miles), which is entered by St. Ninian's Road and Port Street.

Stirling, a county town and an important agricultural centre, is an old royal burgh ("the bulwark of the North") that has played a prominent role in Scottish history. The older part of the town, with irregular streets and many interesting houses, is built on a long ridge climbing above the Forth and culminating in an abrupt crag surmounted by the castle. In the fine 15th-16th century Gothic Church of the Holy Rude (admission weekdays, 10 to 5), Mary, Queen of Scots, was crowned in 1543, at the age of nine months, and her son, James VI (later James I of England) was likewise crowned here, in 1567, John Knox preaching the sermon. In Castle Wynd, which ascends to the broad esplanade, are the unfinished Mar's Wark, a town house begun about 1570 for the Earl of Mar, and the Argyll Lodging, built about 1630 for the 1st Earl of Stirling, founder of Nova Scotia, and afterwards the possession of the Marquesses of Argyll, who enlarged the charming courtyard (1674). The Castle (admission 10 to 6.45, Sundays 11 to 6; October-March 10 to 4, Sundays 1 to 4), in an almost impregnable position on the summit of its precipitous rock, is reached through a Counterguard, mainly of the 18th century, and a 15th century gatehouse. The chief buildings, grouped round a square, are the Great Hall, erected about 1475 for James III; the Chapel Royal, rebuilt in 1594 for James VI; and the Palace, rebuilt in 1539 for James V, with a remarkable façade showing early Renaissance features introduced from France. In the west wing is the Museum of the Argyll and Sutherland Highlanders, who are garrisoned in the castle. The ramparts of the Nether Bailey, at the north end, command a wonderful view of the guardians of the Highlands, from Ben Lomond to Ben Vorlich. Below Castle Wynd, in Broad Street, is the Old Tolbooth (1701), now the Scottish Tartans Information Centre (admission weekdays, 2 to 5, in summer; also 10.30 to 12.30 on Saturdays). The Smith Institute (admission weekdays, 10 to 5), below the castle rock on the south, includes an interesting historical museum.

A84 across the Carse (i.e. plain) of Stirling, passing south of Blair Drummond (5 miles), to Kincardine ($\frac{1}{2}$ mile).

Blair Drummond, rebuilt in 1868, is a mansion (with fine gardens, open occasionally) of the Drummond family, whose monuments are in Kincardine Church (1814), north of the road junction.

A873 on through Thornhill ($3\frac{1}{2}$ miles), then A81 on to Port of Menteith (5 miles).

Port of Menteith is a small village below the Menteith Hills and at the north-east angle of the Lake of Menteith. On an islet (reached by boat from the landing near the church) are the ruins of Inchmahome Priory (admission April-mid November, 10 to 4 or 7; Sundays from 2), founded in the 13th century for Augustinian canons.

A81 on, north of the lake, for $3\frac{1}{2}$ miles, then A821 to Aberfoyle (1 mile more).

Aberfoyle is a suburbanised village in a beautiful position below the end of the Menteith Hills, on the Highland Fault, which marks the geological division between the Highlands and the Lowlands. The plough coulter hanging from a tree opposite the Bailie Nicol Jarvie Hotel recalls a famous scene in Scott's *Rob Roy*. The road (B829) going on from Aberfoyle leads past Loch Ard, on the north side of the Queen Elizabeth Forest Park, to the isthmus between Loch Katrine and Inversnaid, on Loch Lomond.

A821 north, climbs steeply across a range of hills, with charming views, then descending to the west end of Loch Achray, from which a road runs west through The Trossachs to the foot of Loch Katrine ($5\frac{1}{2}$ miles).

The Trossachs, among the most beautiful parts of Scotland (but greatly over-crowded in the height of summer), are a restricted gorge strewn with rocks and filled with a luxuriant growth of varied trees and plants. They extend from the small but lovely Loch Achray to the pier at the east end of Loch Katrine (steamer cruises in summer), an enchanting lake first made famous by Scott's

11

romantic poem, ' The Lady of the Lake '. A footway on the north side affords a delightful view of the rugged Ben Venue, and of Ben Lomond and the peaks beyond Loch Lomond.

A821 on the north side of Loch Achray to Brig o' Turk (2 miles) and thence along the shore of Loch Venachar.

Brig o' Turk is a hamlet between the two lochs, at the foot of Glen Finglas. Loch Venachar is beautifully situated between the Menteith Hills and the pyramid-shaped Ben Ledi.

A821 on from the road junction for 1 mile, then A84 (left) through the Pass of Leny to the foot of Loch Lubnaig (2 miles), whose east shore it follows nearly to Strathyre (5 miles).

The Pass of Leny is a constricted and wood-filled passage forced by the Leny between the slopes of Ben Ledi and Ben Vorlich. Loch Lubnaig is a sombre lake 4 miles long, hemmed in by steep hillsides clothed in dark woods. Strathyre, to the north, is a small village and angling resort in the deep glen of the same name.

A84 on to the Kingshouse Inn (2 miles) and thence to Lochearnhead (3 miles).

Balquhidder, 2 miles west of the Kingshouse Inn on a by-road, is a pleasant village at the head of Strathyre and the foot of Loch Voil. Robert MacGregor, the notorious freebooter made famous by Scott's novel, *Rob Roy*, is almost certainly buried in the churchyard, but the three tombstones in front of the ruined Old Church (1631), claimed to be those of Rob Roy, his wife and two of his sons, date from long before his time. The road goes on along the north shore of the charming Loch Voil, above which rise the Braes of Balquhidder, in the heart of the MacGregor country, to Inverlochlarig (6 miles), on the site of the house in which Rob Roy died in 1734. Lochearnhead is a village and favourite water-sports resort, facing down the steep-sided loch, above which Ben Vorlich rises proudly to the south.

A85 along the north shore of Loch Earn to St. Fillans (6½ miles).

St. Fillans is a delightful village and a sailing centre at the foot of the loch, from which the river Earn emerges.

A85 on through Strathearn to Comrie (5½ miles).

Comrie is a small town and summer resort, finely situated in the strath of the Earn at the junction of Glen Artney (to the south) and Glen Lednock. A shady path ascends the Lednock for ¾-mile to the De'il's Cauldron, a rock chasm through which the river forces its way.

A85 on through the beautiful strath of the Earn to Crieff (6½ miles).

Crieff is a thriving market town and a favourite summer resort, a gateway to the Perthshire Highlands. In the High Street are the Town Hall (1665), with the old iron stocks outside, the Cross of the Burgh of Regality of the Drummonds (1688), who held sway over Strathearn, and the Burgh Cross, perhaps of the 10th century. The Knock, to the north of the town, is a heather-topped ridge that affords a splendid view over the strath and its enclosing mountains, with the Ochils to the south.

A822 south, passing the fine avenue leading to Drummond Castle ($2\frac{1}{2}$ miles), and going on to Muthill (1 mile).

Drummond Castle (admission early April to mid-August, Wednesdays and Saturdays, 2 to 6, to the beautiful terraced gardens), is a mansion partly of the 17th century, but enlarged after a fire in 1898. In the grounds is the restored 15th century Old Keep, which now contains an armoury. Muthill has the ruins of an early-15th century church with a square 12th century tower.

A822 on for $1\frac{1}{2}$ miles, then A823 (left) to Tullibardine (3 miles) and thence to Gleneagles (1 mile more).

Tullibardine Chapel (key at the near-by farm), $\frac{1}{4}$-mile left of the road, was built in 1446 as a collegiate church by Sir David Murray. Unrestored, except for the timber roof, it is now the mausoleum of the Earls of Perth. Gleneagles, in a moorland situation between Strathearn and the head of Strathallan, is a famous golfing resort with a fashionable course, a huge hotel, a railway station, but no village.

A823 on up Glen Eagles, crossing the watershed of the Ochil Hills at 881 feet, then down to Glendevon (5 miles).

Glen Eagles is a steep-sided valley on the north side of the Ochils. Glendevon is a pleasant village in the glen of the same name, with a well-restored tower-house higher up.

A823 on to the Yetts of Muckart ($2\frac{1}{2}$ miles) and thence to Rumbling Bridge ($1\frac{1}{2}$ miles).

The Yetts of Muckart (i.e. ' Gates ') are an important cross-roads at the southern foot of the Ochils. At Rumbling Bridge the river Devon pushes its way through a deep and narrow ravine, forming charming cascades.

A823 on to Powmill (1 mile) and thence over the moorland Cleish Hills (1,243 feet) to Dunfermline ($9\frac{1}{2}$ miles).

Dunfermline is described in Tour 3 (page 21).

A823 on past Rosyth ($2\frac{1}{2}$ miles), then M90 (right) and its continuation A90 across the Forth Road Bridge (see Tour 2, page 15) to the Queensferry roundabout ($4\frac{1}{2}$ miles); the town itself is avoided by this road.

Rosyth has a large ' garden city ' serving the royal dockyard and naval base.

A90 on to Cramond Bridge (4 miles; on Tour 2) and thence to Edinburgh ($5\frac{1}{2}$ miles more), which is entered by Queensferry Road and Dean Bridge.

To Pitlochry

Ballinluig
A827

Grandtully

Aberfeldy
A9

Fortingall

A827
Kenmore

Fearnan
A827

Dunkeld

Birnam

Lawers

Loch Tay

A9

Killin
A827

Lix Toll

A85

Lochearnhead

A84   Loch Earn

Kingshouse Inn

Strathyre

Perth

A90

Bridge of Earn

Loch Lubnaig

A84

Pass of Leny

Aberar

Callander

A84

Glenfarg
A90

Milnathort

Doune
A820   **Dunblane**

A9

Bridge of Allan

A907

Causewayhead

Alloa

Stirling

Kinross

Loc
Le

Cowdenb

A907

Clackmannan

A907

A977

Dunfermline

A994

Crossgat

Culross

A90

Kincardine

0005

Cairneyhill

M90

Rosyth

Firt
Fo

A90

River Forth

Forth Road Bridge

Queensfer

A90

Cramond Bridge

Edinb

Tour 2
174miles

▮▮▮▮▮▮▮▮▮▮▮▮▮▮▮▮▮▮▮▮▮▮▮

Unclassified Roads

△
N

2. The Forth and the Teith, Strathtay and Perth

This tour, starting (like Tours 1 and 3) at Edinburgh, crosses the Forth by the new road bridge at Queensferry and takes in Culross, a fascinating old town with a wealth of unspoiled houses, and the dominating Wallace Monument near Stirling. From Dunblane, a charming small city with an interesting cathedral, it ascends the vale of the Teith, passing Callander, and takes in the lochs of Lubnaig and Earn and the equally beautiful Loch Tay, which has the old villages of Killin and Kenmore at either end. The route descends the long strath of the Tay, by way of Aberfeldy, a noted tourist centre, and Dunkeld, another small city, delightfully situated, with well-restored rows of old houses, to reach the 'Fair City' of Perth, from which it returns over the Ochil Hills and through Kinross, on the shores of Loch Leven, now a wildlife sanctuary.

From Edinburgh (Princes Street) by A90 via Queensferry Road to Cramond Bridge ($5\frac{1}{2}$ miles) and thence to the Queensferry roundabout (4 miles).

Cramond Bridge is a residential suburb of Edinburgh, with a 17th century bridge over the Almond, at the mouth of which, on the Firth of Forth, is the delightful old village of Cramond. Queensferry (Tour 3, page 24) is avoided by the main road.

A90 on across the Forth Road Bridge (toll) to its continuation M90, then A985 (left) to Rosyth ($4\frac{1}{2}$ miles).

The Forth Road Bridge, built in 1958-64 over the Firth, has the longest suspended span in Britain (3,300 feet), and the roadway is supported by 30,000 miles of wire spliced together in cables over 22 inches in diameter. The Forth Railway Bridge, downstream, is an engineering masterpiece built in 1883-90 on the cantilever system. Rosyth has a large 'garden city' serving the Naval Base, founded in 1903, and the Dockyard, the only one in Britain for servicing nuclear submarines.

A985 on to Cairneyhill ($5\frac{1}{2}$ miles), where A994 comes in from Dunfermline (on Tour 1), then by an unclassified road (left) to Culross (3 miles).

Culross, on the steep shore of the Firth of Forth, is the most perfect example of a small Scottish town of the 16th-17th centuries, with many interesting whitewashed houses and narrow cobbled streets and alleys, carefully restored by the National Trust for Scotland. The so-called Palace (admission 10 to 7; October-March to 4; Sundays from 2) is a delightful mansion (with painted rooms) built in 1597-1611 for Sir George Bruce, who first developed the town. In the centre of the 'new town' is The Study (admission daily, except Sunday mornings, 10 to 12.30 and 2 to 7.30; October-March to 4.30), built about 1600, with a corbelled-out turret containing an outlook chamber, and a room devoted to local history. In the upper part of the town is Culross Abbey (admission as for the Palace), a 13th century Cistercian foundation of which the choir and transepts now form the parish church. In a chamber opening off the north transept is the alabaster monument (1642) of Sir George Bruce and his family.

Unclassified road on to Kincardine (5 miles), then A977 (right) for 2 miles and A907 (left) to Clackmannan (1½ miles more).

Kincardine is a small town on the Forth, which is crossed by a bridge built in 1936, with a central swing span of 100 yards. Clackmannan, now hardly more than a village, stands on a hill and has several interesting buildings, including a Tolbooth tower of 1592.

A907 on to Alloa (2 miles) and thence to Causewayhead (5½ miles), where A9 comes in from Stirling (on Tour 1).

Alloa, a manufacturing town on the broadening Forth, is the county town of Clackmannanshire, the smallest county in Scotland. The 15th century Alloa Tower was a stronghold of the powerful Erskines, Earls of Mar. Causewayhead, a suburb of Stirling, is at the foot of the Abbey Craig, a steep-faced wooded hill surmounted by the Wallace Monument (admission daily, 10 to 7.30 or dusk), a tower 220 feet high in the Scottish baronial style (1869), commemorating Sir William Wallace, the patriot, who in 1297 defeated the English near Stirling Bridge, over the Forth. The lantern at the top of the tower commands a famous view that includes Stirling Castle on its rock and the outposts of the Highlands.

A9 north to Bridge of Allan (1½ miles).

Bridge of Allan is a favoured summer resort and a former spa on the Allan Water, in a wooded setting below the west flanks of the Ochil Hills.

A9 on to Dunblane.

Dunblane is a delightful small city at the foot of Strathallan. The Gothic Cathedral (admission 10 to 7; October-March to 4; Sundays 2 to 5.30 or 4), mainly of the 13th century, has a Norman tower, a fine west front praised by Ruskin, and a graceful nave. In the choir is the tomb-slab of Margaret Drummond, the wife (though not the queen) of James IV; she was poisoned at Drummond Castle by nobles who sought an alliance of the king with Princess Margaret Tudor. In the High Street are the 17th century Dean's House (admission weekdays, 10.30 to 12.30 and 2.30 to 4.30), now the cathedral museum, and the Leighton Library, founded in 1688 by Robert Leighton, later Archbishop of Glasgow.

A820 west of the Allan Water to Doune (4 miles).

Doune, once famous for the manufacture of pistols, is a small town on the swiftly-flowing Teith. Doune Castle (admission daily, 10 to 6 or dusk; closed in December and on Thursdays, except in May-

16

September) is a fine example (though in ruins) of a Scottish medieval stronghold, built in the 15th century and given by James IV to his queen, Margaret Tudor.

A84 on to Callander (8 miles).

Callander is a pleasant town and a tourist resort, a ' gateway to the Highlands ' and the starting point for the round of The Trossachs, with a fine view of Ben Ledi from the bridge over the Teith.

A84 on through the Pass of Leny to the foot of Loch Lubnaig ($3\frac{1}{2}$ miles), whose east shore it follows nearly to Strathyre (5 miles).

The Pass of Leny is a constricted and wood-filled passage forced by the Leny between the slopes of Ben Ledi and Ben Vorlich. Loch Lubnaig is a sombre lake 4 miles long, hemmed in by steep hillsides clothed in dark woods. Strathyre, to the north, is a small village and angling resort in the deep glen of the same name.

A84 on to the Kingshouse Inn (2 miles) and thence to Lochearnhead (3 miles).

Balquhidder, 2 miles west of the Kingshouse Inn on a by-road, is described in Tour 1 (page 12). Lochearnhead is a village and favourite water-sports resort, facing down the steep-sided loch, above which Ben Vorlich rises proudly to the south.

A85 north up the wild rock-strewn Glen Ogle, crossing the watershed at 945 feet, then descending steeply to Lix Toll (5 miles), in Glen Dochart, through which A827 leads to Killin ($2\frac{1}{2}$ miles).

Killin is a pleasant village and a popular summer resort between the Dochart and the Lochay, which join forces just before entering Loch Tay. Above the old Bridge of 1760, the Falls of Dochart rush down in foaming cascades.

A827 on above the north shore of Loch Tay to Lawers ($8\frac{1}{2}$ miles), then descending to the lake before Fearnan ($4\frac{1}{2}$ miles).

Loch Tay, famous for its salmon, is $14\frac{1}{2}$ miles long and over 500 feet deep, but only $\frac{3}{4}$-mile wide. It is dominated on the north by Ben Lawers, remarkable for its alpine flowers and a favoured ski-ing ground. From Fearnan a road runs north to Fortingall ($2\frac{1}{2}$ miles), a model village at the foot of the long Glen Lyon.

A827 on, following the shore under the wooded Drummond Hill to Kenmore ($3\frac{1}{2}$ miles).

Kenmore is another model village, with charming whitewashed cottages, at the foot of the loch, from which the river Tay issues. Taymouth Castle, to the east, is an early-19th century mansion in a beautiful wooded park with a golf-course.

A827 on through the delightful strath of the Tay to Aberfeldy (6 miles).

Aberfeldy is an old market town and a holiday resort on the Tay. The Black Watch, a regiment founded here in 1739 to keep watch on the Highlanders, is commemorated by a monument near the

Tay Bridge, built in 1733 by William Adam for General Wade, the road builder, and crossing the river for Weem, a hamlet with a charming inn, beyond which is Castle Menzies, an excellent example of a 16th century Scottish mansion.

A827 on past Grandtully Castle to Grandtully ($4\frac{1}{2}$ miles), where the Tay is crossed, and thence to Ballinluig ($5\frac{1}{4}$ miles).

Grandtully Castle is a fine baronial mansion of the Stewarts, mainly of the 16th-17th centuries, and one of the supposed originals of ' Tullyveolan ' in Scott's *Waverley*. The 16th century St. Mary's Church, $\frac{1}{2}$-mile south, has a finely-painted wooden ceiling. Ballinluig is a village on the Tummel above its junction with the Tay.

A9 down the beautiful Strathtay to Dunkeld ($7\frac{1}{2}$ miles) and thence across the river to Birnam (1 mile).

Dunkeld is a tiny city (though not a burgh) in a delightful position on a broad reach of the Tay, enclosed between richly-wooded crags. The Cathedral (admission 10 to 7; October-March to 4; Sundays from 2), founded in the 12th century and desecrated in 1560, consists of a ruined 15th century nave and a restored 13th-14th century choir (now the parish church) containing a 14th century effigy said to represent Alexander Stewart, the notorious ' Wolf of Badenoch '. In Cathedral Street and High Street are charming rows of whitewashed houses carefully restored by the National Trust for Scotland. A fine bridge by Thomas Telford (1809) crosses the river for Birnam, a pleasant village and small summer resort below Birnam Hill, which affords a wide view over Strath Tay to the Sidlaw Hills, to the south-east, including Dunsinane, $12\frac{1}{2}$ miles away, to which Birnam Wood ' marched ' in *Macbeth*.

A9 on through the Pass of Birnam, a ' gateway to the Highlands ', and thence to Perth ($13\frac{1}{2}$ miles).

Perth, often called the ' Fair City ', is an old royal burgh, and a historic county town and thriving agricultural centre, enclosed by delightfully wooded hills. The capital of Scotland from its foundation in 1210 by William the Lion until the 15th century, it is well situated between the large meadows of the North and South Inch, on the broad Tay, which is crossed by an 18th century bridge by John Smeaton. The Art Gallery and Museum (admission 10 to 1 and 2 to 5; Tuesdays and Fridays also 6 to 8; Sundays 2 to 4), in George Street, has good collections illustrating the history and natural history of Perthshire. Near by is the Fair Maid's House, said to be that described in Scott's novel, *The Fair Maid of Perth*. St. John's Church (admission Monday-Friday 11 to 1 and 2 to 4; Saturdays 10 to 12 and 2 to 4) is a fine Gothic building of the 15th century. Here in 1559 John Knox preached his famous iconoclastic sermon that urged " the purging of the churches from idolatry ".

A90 south, leaving Perth by Edinburgh Road and crossing the ridge of Moncreiffe Hill to Bridge of Earn ($3\frac{1}{2}$ miles), and thence across a plain to Aberargie (3 miles); then up Glen Farg to the village of Glenfarg (4½ miles).

Bridge of Earn is a small summer resort and angling centre on the Earn, near the east end of its wide strath. Glenfarg is at the head of a delightful ravine in the northern slopes of the Ochil Hills.

A90 on to Milnathort (4½ miles).

Milnathort is a small agricultural town to the north-west of Loch Leven. Burleigh Castle (key at the farm opposite), ½-mile east, is a fine 16th century tower-house of the Balfours.

A90 on to Kinross (2 miles).

Kinross is a quiet county town and a favourite angling resort on the west side of Loch Leven, most of the shores of which are now a nature reserve. On a peninsula is Kinross House, built for himself about 1685 by Sir William Bruce, who introduced classical architecture into Scotland, and on an island (reached by ferry boat), ¼-mile offshore, is Lochleven Castle, famous for the escape from imprisonment here in 1568 of Mary, Queen of Scots.

A90 on to Cowdenbeath (7 miles), in the centre of a colliery district, and thence to Crossgates (2½ miles). A90 and its continuation M90 on to the Forth Road Bridge, from which Edinburgh (17 miles) is reached by the outgoing route.

To Bridge of Cally

Rattray

A923

Blairgowrie

Dunkeld

A9

A822

Meikleour

A93

Milton

Amulree

Stobhall

Newton Bridge

Sma' Glen

A822

Scone Palace

A93

Gilmerton

A9

Crieff

A85

A822

Perth

Muthill

B9112

Drummond Castle

B934

Forteviot

A822

Dunning

Braco

Greenloaning

Hills

A9

Ochil

B934

Yetts of Muckart

Dunblane

Rumbling Bridge

Bridge of Allan

A823

Powmill

Causewayhead

Cleish Hills

A9

A907

Alloa

Stirling

Clackmannan

Dunfermline

A977

Kincardine

A823

A876

Rosyth

River Forth

Forth Road Bridge

A905

Bo'ness

Firth of Fo

A90

Grangemouth

The Binns

A904

Kinneil House

Queensferry

B924

A90

Edinb

Falkirk

A9

A904

Hopetoun House

B924

A90

Cramond Bridge

Tour 3
159 miles

N

3. Dunfermline, Perth, Strathallan and the Forth

This tour, likewise starting from Edinburgh (see Tour 1), takes in the historic city of Dunfermline, with its fine abbey church, the burial-place of Robert Bruce, and the 'Fair City' of Perth, once the capital of Scotland. It goes past Scone Palace, an interesting house on an ancient site, to Blairgowrie, a 'gateway' to the eastern Grampians, then turns along the foothills to Dunkeld, a tiny city delightfully situated in Strathtay, from which it crosses to Crieff, a favourite tourist centre and another gateway to the Highlands. From here, the route descends Strathallan through Dunblane, another small city with a notable cathedral. Crossing the Forth at Kincardine, it returns on the south side by way of Queensferry, an old port from which the splendid classical mansion of Hopetoun House may be visited.

From Edinburgh (Princes Street) to the Queensferry roundabout ($9\frac{1}{2}$ miles), see Tour 2. A 90 on across the Forth Road Bridge to its continuation M90, then A823 (left) to Dunfermline (7 miles).

Dunfermline is a historic city and royal burgh, long favoured as a residence of the Scottish kings, many of whom were born or are buried here. The Abbey Church (admission 10 to 7; October-March to 4; Sundays from 2, except during service) was originally that of a Benedictine priory founded about 1070 by St. Margaret, the Saxon queen of Malcolm Canmore, and raised to the rank of abbey by David I. Of the new church consecrated in 1150, there survives the splendid Norman nave, one of the finest examples of Romanesque architecture in Scotland. In the choir, rebuilt in 1822 in place of that pulled down at the Reformation, is the grave of King Robert Bruce, beneath a modern memorial brass. Dunfermline is the headquarters of the Carnegie Trusts, founded in 1903 by Andrew Carnegie, the millionaire and philanthropist, whose humble cottage birthplace (admission weekdays, 11 to 1 and 2 to 6 or 8; Sundays 2 to 6) is down the steep hill from the church. Carnegie gave many buildings to the city, as well as the beautiful Pittencrieff Glen, with the 17th century house, now a museum of local history, and the ruins of the royal Palace (rebuilt by James IV in 1500), where Charles I was born in 1600.

A823 on over the moorland Cleish Hills (1,243 feet) to Rumbling Bridge ($10\frac{1}{2}$ miles) and thence to the Yetts of Muckhart ($1\frac{1}{2}$ miles).

Rumbling Bridge. Here the river Devon forces its way through a deep and narrow ravine, with charming cascades. The Yetts of Muckhart (i.e. 'Gates') are important cross-roads at the southern foot of the Ochil Hills.

A823 on for $\frac{1}{2}$-mile, then B934 (right) up the steep valley of the Glendey Burn (a tributary of the Devon), crossing the summit ridge of the Ochils at 1,038 feet before descending to Dunning (9 miles more).

Dunning, at the northern foot of the steep-faced Ochil Hills, has a rebuilt church with an early-13th century tower.

B934 on across Strathearn to Forteviot ($2\frac{1}{2}$ miles) and thence over the Earn ($\frac{1}{2}$-mile more); then B9112 (right), skirting the wooded estate of the demolished Dupplin Castle and joining A9 before reaching Perth (6 miles).

Perth is described in Tour 2 (page 18).

A93 across the Tay, then north, skirting the fine park of Scone Palace, to Old Scone ($2\frac{1}{2}$ miles).

Scone Palace (admission Easter-mid-October; weekdays, except Friday, 11 to 5; Sundays 2 to 5) is an early-19th century Gothic mansion containing notable paintings, ivories, furniture, and porcelain. It stands on the site of a 12th century abbey destroyed by a mob inflamed by the iconoclastic sermon of John Knox at Perth. Scone had been an important meeting place since the 8th century, and to it, in about 850, Kenneth Macalpine, the first king of a united Scotland, brought the 'Stone of Scone', said to carry sovereignty with it. Edward I carried the stone off to London in 1297 (it is now in Westminster Abbey), but all the kings of Scotland until James I (1406) continued to be crowned at Scone. James IV also was crowned here (in 1488), as was Charles II, in 1651.

A93 on past Stobhall (5 miles) and across the Isla to Meikleour ($4\frac{1}{2}$ miles).

Stobhall, above the wooded east bank of the Tay, is the 16th-17th century house of the Earl of Perth. Near Meikleour the road runs alongside a magnificent beech hedge, nearly 600 yards long, planted about 1746 and now over 85 feet high.

A93 on over the fertile vale of Strathmore to Blairgowrie (4 miles).

Blairgowrie is a pleasant market town and a summer and angling resort, with extensive raspberry fields. It stands on the west bank of the Ericht, below the point where the river emerges from the Grampians through a rugged gorge. Bridge of Cally (see Tour 10, page 62) is 6 miles north by A93, which ascends through the gorge from Rattray, on the east bank.

A923 west below the foothills of the Grampians, passing a chain of quiet lochs fed by the Lunan, and joining A9 $\frac{1}{2}$-mile north of Dunkeld ($11\frac{1}{2}$ miles).

Dunkeld is described in Tour 2 (page 18).

A9 across the Tay to Little Dunkeld ($\frac{1}{2}$ mile), then A822 through the pleasant Strathbraan to Milton (7 miles), and thence to Amulree (2 miles).

Inver. B898, on the right, beyond the road junction at Little Dunkeld, leads to Inver, with the cottage of the Gows, three generations of fiddlers. Beyond the hamlet is The Hermitage, a charming stretch of woodland near a waterfall on the Braan, best seen from Ossian's Hall, an 18th century belvedere. Amulree is a small village among heather-clad moorlands, on the Braan, at the foot of Glen Quaich.

A822 on to Newton Bridge (4 miles) and then through the Sma' Glen and on to Gilmerton (6½ miles).

The Sma' Glen (i.e. Small), actually part of Glen Almond, is a rock and heather ravine, 2½ miles long, the road through which was first made by General Wade in 1746, after the second Jacobite rising.

A85 (right) to Crieff (2 miles).

Crieff is described in Tour 1 (page 12).

A822 south, passing the fine avenue leading to Drummond Castle (2½ miles), and thence to Muthill (1 mile).

Drummond Castle (admission early April to mid-August, Wednesdays and Saturdays, 2 to 6, to the beautiful terraced gardens), is a mansion partly of the 17th century, but enlarged after a fire in 1898. In the grounds is the restored 15th century Old Keep, which now contains an armoury. Muthill has the ruins of an early-15th century church with a square 12th century tower.

A822 on to Braco (6 miles), to the north of which are the impressive earthworks of a large Roman fort, and then to Greenloaning (1½ miles); then A9 (right) through Strathallan to Dunblane (5½ miles).

Dunblane is described in Tour 2 (page 16).

A9 on to Bridge of Allan (2½ miles) and thence to Causewayhead (1½ miles).

Bridge of Allan is a favoured summer resort and a former spa on the Allan Water, in a wooded setting below the west flanks of the Ochil Hills. Causewayhead, a suburb of Stirling (on Tour 1), is at the foot of the Abbey Craig, a steep-faced wooded hill surmounted by the Wallace Monument (admission daily, 10 to 7.30 or dusk), a tower 220 feet high in the Scottish baronial style (1869), commemorating Sir William Wallace, the patriot, who in 1297 defeated the English near Stirling Bridge, over the Forth. The lantern at the top of the tower commands a famous view that includes Stirling Castle on its rock and the outposts of the Highlands.

A907 east to Alloa (5½ miles) and thence to Clackmannan (2 miles).

Alloa, a manufacturing town on the broadening Forth, is the county town of Clackmannanshire, the smallest county in Scotland. The 15th century Alloa Tower was a stronghold of the powerful Erskines, Earls of Mar. Clackmannan, now hardly more than a village, stands on a hill and has several interesting buildings, including a Tolbooth tower of 1592.

A907 on for 2 miles, then A977 (right) to Kincardine (2 miles).

Kincardine is a small town on the Forth, which is crossed by a bridge built in 1936, with a central swing span of 100 yards.

A876 across the river and on for 3 miles, then A905 (left) for 2 miles, and A904 (left again) to Grangemouth (1 mile).

Grangemouth is a rapidly-expanding port with huge oil-refineries, chemical works, and shipbuilding and timber yards, at the mouth of the Carron in the Firth of Forth.

A904 on below Kinneil House (4 miles) and thence to Bo'ness (1 mile).

Kinneil House (admission 10 to 7; October-March 12 to 4; Sundays from 2) is a 16th century mansion, formerly of the Dukes of Hamilton, with contemporary wall paintings. Bo'ness (a contraction of Borrowstounness) is an industrial town on the Firth of Forth.

A904 on south of The Binns (4½ miles).

The Binns (admission Saturdays and Sundays throughout the year, daily from mid-June to mid-September; 2 to 5); is a house of the 15th century and later, with ornate 17th century plaster ceilings and relics of General 'Tam' Dalyell, commander of the royalist forces in Scotland, who raised the Royal Scots Greys here in 1681.

A904 on for 4½ miles, then B924 (left) to Queensferry (1 mile).

Queensferry (or South Queensferry) is an old town and a royal burgh on the shore of the firth, named from Margaret, queen of Malcolm Canmore, and from its ferry, superseded by the Forth Road Bridge (see page 15), of which it affords a striking view. The Episcopalian Church was originally the chapel of a 14th century Carmelite friary. The 17th century Hawes Inn, opposite the pier, ½-mile east, plays a part in Scott's *The Antiquary* and Stevenson's *Kidnapped*. Hopetoun House (admission May-September, daily, except Thursdays and Fridays, 1.30 to 5.45), 2 miles west, the magnificent seat of the Marquess of Linlithgow, was mainly built in the 18th century by William Adam and his sons.

B924 on past the Hawes Inn (see above) and under the Forth Railway Bridge, then skirting Dalmeny Park to join A90 (2½ miles), which enters Edinburgh (7 miles more) by the outgoing route.

4. Loch Long and Loch Fyne, Loch Awe and Loch Lomond

This and the next two tours start from Glasgow and they cover much of the south and south-west parts of the Central Highlands. This route takes in five varied and well-known lochs, the inland lakes of Loch Awe and Loch Lomond and the fjords of Loch Goil, Loch Long and Loch Fyne, as well as the mountainous country around the Strath of Orchy and Strath Fillan. It also includes Dumbarton, an ancient capital with a royal fortress on a precipitous rock, the summer resorts of Helensburgh, on the Clyde estuary, and Arrochar, which commands a magnificent view of the Ben Arthur range of mountains, and the delightful town of Inveraray, with its splendid baronial castle of the Campbell chiefs.

From Glasgow (Buchanan Street) by Cowcaddens Street and A82, avoiding the industrial areas along the Clyde, to Milton (12½ miles), then A814 (left) to Dumbarton (1½ miles).

Dumbarton, an historic royal burgh and county town, is a thriving industrial centre at the foot of the Vale of Leven. On an isolated rock, rising abruptly from the bank of the Clyde, is the Castle (admission 10 to 7, October-March to 4; Sundays from 2), a royal stronghold since the 13th century, though the surviving buildings are mainly of the 17th and 18th centuries. The summit of the rock, reached by a long flight of steps, commands a view over the Clyde estuary and to the frontiers of the Highlands.

A814 on to Cardross (4 miles) and thence via Craigendoran to Helensburgh (4½ miles).

Helensburgh, on the north shore of the estuary, is a pleasant residential town and a favourite summer resort, named after the wife of Sir James Colquhoun of Luss, for whom it was laid out on the chequer-board plan after 1776. The pier at Craigendoran, to the east, is a popular starting point of steamers to the Firth of Clyde and the neighbouring lochs.

A814 on to Rhu (2 miles) and thence along the east shore of the Gare Loch via Faslane Bay (4 miles) to Garelochhead (1½ miles).

Rhu is a yachting resort inside the narrow mouth of the Gare Loch, a sea-loch 6 miles long, opening off the Firth of Clyde and also put to commercial and naval use. The British Polaris submarine base was completed here, at Faslane Bay, in 1968. Garelochhead is a village and small resort at the upper end of the loch.

A814 ascends steeply to Whistlefield (1½ miles), then drops down to Finnart (1½ miles), on the east shore of Loch Long.

Whistlefield, on the watershed between the two lochs, commands a charming view of the entrance to Loch Goil, to the west, and the Argyll mountains around it. Loch Long, over 17 miles in length,

Tour 4
145 miles

N

Loch Awe

Glen Lochy
A85

A85
Dalmally

A819
Cladich

A819

Dundarave
Glen A83 Castle
Aray
Cairndow
A83
Inveraray
Rest & Be
Thankful
A83
Glen Croe
Ardgartan
Arrochar

A814
Loch Fyne
A82
Loch Goil
Luss
Loch Lomond

Loch Long
A814
Rhu
Gare
Loch
Helensburgh
Balloch
Cardross
Alexandria
Firth of Clyde
A814
A82
Dumbarton
Milton

A82

Glasgow

Tyndrum
A82

Crianlarich

Glen Falloch

Ardlui
A82

Inveruglas

Tarbet

Whistlefield
Garelochhead

is one of the deepest and most beautiful sea-lochs in Scotland, and is used for submarine trials. The road through the woods along the shore affords views of the rugged mountains of Ardgoil, or 'Argyll's Bowling Green', on the opposite shore of the loch.

A814 on, following the shore of Loch Long, to Arrochar (7 miles).

Arrochar is a village and popular holiday resort beautifully situated near the head of the loch, with a wonderful view of the forked peak of Ben Arthur, usually called the Cobbler, and other grand heights of its range.

A83 round the head of the loch, crossing the foot of Glen Loin, to Ardgartan ($2\frac{1}{2}$ miles), then ascending Glen Croe to Rest and be Thankful ($4\frac{1}{2}$ miles).

Ardgartan, at the mouth of the Croe in Loch Long, has a large camping ground in Ardgartan Forest, part of the Argyll National Forest Park. Glen Croe, once wild and desolate, is now partly afforested. The road through it ascends steadily across the south side of Ben Arthur, above the old road, which keeps mainly to the valley bottom, then climbs in steep zigzags to the summit of the pass (860 feet) near a stone seat inscribed 'Rest and be Thankful', from which there is an impressive view.

A83 on down Glen Kinglas to Cairndow (5 miles) on the shore of Loch Fyne.

Loch Fyne, 42 miles long, is one of the largest sea-lochs in Scotland, and has long been famous for its herrings.

A83 round the head of Loch Fyne to Dundarave Castle ($5\frac{1}{2}$ miles).

Dundarave Castle, on the upper reach of the loch, is a restored 16th century tower-house of the Macnachtons, the 'Doom Castle' of Neil Munro's novel of that name.

A83 on, beside Loch Fyne, to Inveraray (5 miles).

Inveraray, near the inlet of Loch Shira and the mouth of the charming Glen Shira, is a small but historic royal burgh laid out on a new site after 1743, and largely and successfully rebuilt in 1957-61 for the Ministry of Works. At the north end of the main street is a fine Celtic cross brought from Iona, and at the other end is the classical Church (1794), divided into two identical parts for services in English and Gaelic. The Courthouse (1820), to the east, is now a centre for training young people in Highland crafts. Crombie's Land, a white house facing the loch, was the birthplace of Neil Munro, who laid scenes in *John Splendid* and *The New Road* in the town. Inveraray Castle (admission Easter to mid-October, daily, except Sunday mornings, 10 to 12.30 and 2 to 6; closed on Fridays until the end of June), in a large park near the foot of Glen Aray, is the seat of the Duke of Argyll, the Highlanders' MacCailean Mòr, or MacCallum More, the head of the Clan Campbell. The imposing Scottish baronial mansion, rebuilt in the 18th century, with massive round towers at the corners and a square central tower, has a finely decorated interior containing family portraits by Gainsborough, Ramsay and Raeburn, and historical relics (of Rob Roy and others).

A819 north through the beautiful woods that extend up Glen Aray, then from the summit (675 feet) down to Cladich ($9\frac{1}{2}$ miles) and along the shore of Loch Awe for $5\frac{1}{2}$ miles to its north-east end; then A85 (right) to Dalmally (1 mile).

Loch Awe, some 24 miles long, is one of the largest lochs in Scotland and one of the most delightful. Its head is at the south-west end, from which it originally drained into the sea at Loch Crinan; its waters are now carried away to the north-west through the narrow Pass of Brander, under the magnficent slopes of Ben Cruachan. The road allows a fine view of the mountain and of Kilchurn Castle, on a peninsula, best reached by boat from the village of Lochawe, on the opposite shore (see Tour 7). Dalmally is a scattered village in the charmingly wooded Strath of Orchy, below the junction of Glen Orchy and Glen Lochy, with a majestic view east of the giant steps of Ben Lui.

A85 up the green Glen Lochy, to the north of Ben Lui, and across the watershed to Tyndrum (12 miles), then A82 down Strath Fillan to Crianlarich (5 miles).

Tyndrum is an angling resort well situated at the head of the strath, surrounded by grand mountains, at the junction of the road to Glen Coe and Fort William (Tour 8). Crianlarich is a village and railway centre in an open moorland setting, at the foot of the strath.

A82 south over the watershed and down Glen Falloch to Ardlui (8 miles), at the head of Loch Lomond.

Ardlui, at the foot of the tree-filled Glen Falloch, is surrounded by fine mountains that include Ben Vorlich and Beinn a' Choin. Loch Lomond, nearly 22 miles long, is the largest inland lake in Britain and one of the most beautiful, with steep shores enclosing its narrow upper reach. Inveruglas, which has a power station fed by the waters of Loch Sloy, behind Ben Vorlich, is connected by a passenger ferry with Inversnaid, in the 'Rob Roy' country on the east shore.

A82 on, along the west shore of the loch, to Inveruglas (5 miles) and on to Tarbet (3 miles).

Tarbet is a hamlet with a steamer pier (see below), on the isthmus, only $1\frac{1}{2}$ miles wide, separating the loch from Loch Long at Arrochar. The charmingly wooded shores are dominated by the graceful peak of Ben Lomond, rising on the east side of the water.

A82 on by the loch side (congested in summer) to Luss ($8\frac{1}{2}$ miles) and thence to Balloch (8 miles).

Luss is a model village in an enchanting position on the ' bonny, bonny banks ' of Loch Lomond, which has here widened out and has numerous islands dotting the surface. Balloch is a residential village and a very popular week-end resort beyond the south end of the loch and on the Leven, the banks of which are lined with cabin-cruisers during the summer. A footpath on the west bank leads to the pier, from which steamers ply up Loch Lomond, calling at Balmaha and Rowardennan (on the east shore), Tarbert and Inversnaid, and visiting also the head reach of the loch.

A82 on to Alexandria (1 mile) in the industrialised Vale of Leven, and thence to Milton ($4\frac{1}{2}$ miles); then by the outgoing route to Glasgow ($12\frac{1}{2}$ miles).

N

Fortingall
Aberfeldy
Fearnan
Kenmore
A827
A826
Lawers
A827
Loch Tay
Amulree
M
Killin
A827
Newton Bridge
Glen Dochart
Lix Toll
Sma'Glen
Crianlarich
A85
Gilmerton
A85
Crieff
A82
Drummond Castle
A822
Muthill
Glen Falloch
A822
Ardlui
Braco
A82
Greenloani
Inveruglas
A9
Tarbet
Dunblane
Arrochar
Bridge of Allan
Causewayhead
Loch Lomond
A9
A82
Stirling
Luss
St.Ninian's
Drymen
A875
A809
Fintry
A80
A811
Killearn
B818
A872
Balloch
B834
Denny
Alexandria
Campsie Fells
Castlecary
A82
Milton
Cumbernauld
A82
A80
A8
Glasgow

Tour 5
159 miles

5. Loch Lomond and Strathtay, Strathallan and Stirling

This tour, starting (like Tours 4 and 6) from Glasgow, takes in the delightful inland lake of Loch Lomond and the beautiful Loch Tay, which has the old villages of Killin and Kenmore at either end. It also includes the favourite tourist centres of Aberfeldy, in the strath of the Tay, and Crieff, in that of the Earn, as well as the charming small city of Dunblane, with its interesting cathedral, and the historic town of Stirling, famous for its royal castle, at the upper end of a long steep ridge along which the old town climbs, resembling that of Edinburgh. Other places of diverse interest are the dominating Wallace Monument, commemorating the patriot who opposed Edward I, the renowned field of Bannockburn, a lasting memorial to Scottish tenacity and valour, and the striking New Town of Cumbernauld.

From Glasgow (Buchanan Street) by A82, as in Tour 4, to Milton ($12\frac{1}{2}$ miles), and thence to Alexandria ($4\frac{1}{2}$ miles) and on to Balloch (1 mile).

Alexandria in an industrial town with textile mills in the Vale of Leven, whose waters drain from Loch Lomond into the Clyde. Balloch is a residential village and a very popular week-end resort on the river, the banks of which are lined with cabin-cruisers during the summer. A footpath on the west bank leads to the pier at the south end of Loch Lomond, the largest inland lake in Britain, nearly 22 miles long, and one of the most beautiful. Steamers ply up the loch in summer, calling at Balmaha and Rowardennan (see Tour 6), Tarbet and Inversnaid, and visiting also the head reach.

A82 (congested in summer) on by the west shore of Loch Lomond to Luss (8 miles) and thence to Tarbet ($8\frac{1}{2}$ miles).

Luss is a model village in an enchanting position on the loch, the broad southern part of which has charmingly wooded shores and numerous islands dotting the surface. The view up the loch is dominated by Ben Lomond, which rises steeply from the opposite shore. Tarbet is a hamlet and small summer resort on the isthmus, only $1\frac{1}{2}$ miles wide, separating the loch from the head of Loch Long at Arrochar.

A82 on along the shore to Inveruglas (3 miles) and thence to Ardlui (5 miles), at the head of the loch; then on up Glen Falloch and over the watershed to Crianlarich (8 miles).

Inveruglas, on the narrow upper reach of Loch Lomond, which is enclosed by steep shores, has a power station fed by the waters of Loch Sloy, behind Ben Vorlich. It is connected by passenger ferry with Inversnaid, in the 'Rob Roy' country on the east shore. Ardlui, surrounded by fine mountains, is a hamlet at the foot of the tree-filled Glen Falloch. Crianlarich is a village and railway centre in an open moorland setting, at the lower end of the broad Strath Fillan.

A85 east through Glen Dochart to Lix Toll ($11\frac{1}{2}$ miles), then A827 on to Killin ($2\frac{1}{2}$ miles).

Glen Dochart is an open valley to the south of which rise Ben More and other fine mountains. Killin is a pleasant village and a popular summer resort between the Dochart and the Lochay, which join forces just before entering Loch Tay. Above the old Bridge of 1760, the Falls of Dochart rush down in foaming cascades.

A827 on above the north shore of Loch Tay to Lawers ($8\frac{1}{2}$ miles), then descending to the loch before Fearnan ($4\frac{1}{2}$ miles) and following the shore under the wooded Drummond Hill to Kenmore ($3\frac{1}{2}$ miles).

Loch Tay, famous for its salmon, is $14\frac{1}{2}$ miles long and over 500 feet deep, but only $\frac{3}{4}$-mile wide. It is dominated on the north by Ben Lawers, remarkable for its alpine flowers and a favoured skiing ground. From Fearnan a road runs north to Fortingall ($2\frac{1}{2}$ miles), a model village at the foot of the long Glen Lyon. Kenmore is another model village, with charming whitewashed cottages, at the foot of the loch, from which the river Tay issues. Taymouth Castle, to the east, is an early-19th century mansion in a beautiful wooded park with a golf course.

A827 on through the delightful strath of the Tay to Aberfeldy (6 miles).

Aberfeldy is an old market town and a holiday resort on the Tay. The Black Watch, a regiment founded here in 1739 to keep watch on the Highlanders, is commemorated by a monument near the Tay Bridge, built in 1733 by William Adam for General Wade, the road builder, and crossing the river for Weem, a hamlet with a charming inn, beyond which is Castle Menzies, an excellent example of a 16th century Scottish mansion.

A826 south, climbing steeply on to the moors and reaching a height of 1,306 feet, then descending through Glen Cochill to Milton (9 miles); then A822 (right) to Amulree (2 miles). From the road over the heather-clad moors a wide view opens of the Perthshire Highlands from Ben Lawers and Schichallion to the Forest of Atholl.

Amulree is a small village on the Braan, near the head of its strath and at the foot of Glen Quaich.

A822 on to Newton Bridge (4 miles) and then through the Sma' Glen and on to Gilmerton ($6\frac{1}{2}$ miles).

The Sma' Glen (i.e. Small), actually part of Glen Almond, is a rock and heather ravine, $2\frac{1}{2}$ miles long, the road through which was first made by General Wade in 1746, after the Jacobite rising.

A85 (right) to Crieff (2 miles), in Strathearn.

Crieff is a thriving market town and a favourite summer resort, a gateway to the Perthshire Highlands. In the High Street are the

Town Hall (1665), with the old iron stocks outside, the Cross of the Burgh of Regality of the Drummonds (1688), who held sway over Strathearn, and the Burgh Cross, perhaps of the 10th century. The Knock, to the north of the town, is a heather-topped ridge that affords a splendid view over the strath and its enclosing mountains, with the Ochil Hills to the south.

A822 south, passing the fine avenue leading to Drummond Castle ($2\frac{1}{2}$ miles), and going on to Muthill (1 mile).

Drummond Castle (admission early April to mid-August, Wednesdays and Saturdays, 2 to 6, to the beautiful terraced gardens) is a mansion partly of the 17th century, but enlarged after a fire in 1898. In the grounds is the restored 15th century Old Keep, which now contains an armoury. Muthill has the ruins of an early-15th century church with a square 12th century tower.

A822 on to Braco (6 miles), to the north of which are the impressive earthworks of a large Roman fort, and thence to Greenloaning ($1\frac{1}{2}$ miles); then A9 (right) through Strathallan to Dunblane ($5\frac{1}{2}$ miles).

Dunblane is a delightful small city at the foot of Strathallan. The Gothic Cathedral (admission 10 to 7; October-March to 4; Sundays 2 to 5.30 or 4), mainly of the 13th century, has a partly Norman tower, a fine west front praised by Ruskin, and a graceful nave. In the choir is the tomb-slab of Margaret Drummond, the wife (though not the queen) of James IV; she was poisoned at Drummond Castle by nobles who sought an alliance of the king with Princess Margaret Tudor. In the High Street are the 17th century Dean's House (admission weekdays, 10.30 to 12.30 and 2.30 to 4.30), now the cathedral museum, and the Leighton Library, founded in 1688 by Robert Leighton, later Archbishop of Glasgow.

A9 on to Bridge of Allan ($2\frac{1}{2}$ miles) and thence to Causewayhead ($1\frac{1}{2}$ miles).

Bridge of Allan and Causewayhead are dsecribed in Tour 3 (page 23).

A9 on, crossing the Forth near the old Stirling Bridge, to Stirling ($1\frac{1}{2}$ miles).

Stirling, a county town and an important agricultural centre, is an old royal burgh (" the bulwark of the north ") that has played a prominent role in Scottish history. The older part of the town, with irregular streets and many interesting houses, is built on a long ridge climbing above the river and culminating in an abrupt crag surmounted by the castle. In the fine 15th-16th century Gothic Church of the Holy Rude (admission weekdays, 10 to 5), Mary, Queen of Scots, was crowned in 1543, at the age of nine months, and her son, James VI, was likewise crowned here (1567), John Knox preaching the sermon. In the Castle Wynd, which ascends to the broad esplanade, are the unfinished Mar's Wark, a town house begun about 1570 for the Earl of Mar, and the Argyll Lodging, built about 1630 for the 1st Earl of Stirling, the founder of Nova Scotia, and afterwards the possession of the Marquesses of Argyll, who enlarged the charming courtyard (1674). The Castle (admission 10 to 6.45, Sundays 11 to 6; October-March 10 to 4, Sundays 1 to 4), in an almost impregnable position on the summit of its precipitous rock, is reached through a Counterguard, mainly of the 18th century, and a 15th century gatehouse. The chief buildings, grouped round a square, are the Great Hall, erected about 1475 for James III; the Chapel Royal, rebuilt in 1594 for James VI; and the Palace, rebuilt in 1539 for James V, with a remarkable façade showing early Renaissance features introduced from France. In the west wing is the Museum of the Argyll and Sutherland Highlanders, who are garrisoned in the castle. The ramparts of the Nether Bailey, at the north end, command a wonderful view of the guardians of the Highlands, from Ben Lomond to Ben Vorlich. Below Castle Wynd, in Broad Street, is the Old Tolbooth (1701), now the Scottish Tartans Information Centre (admission weekdays, 2 to 5, in summer; also 10.30 to 12.30 on Saturdays). The Smith Institute (admission weekdays, 10 to 5), below the castle rock on the south, includes an interesting historical museum.

A9 on, leaving Stirling by Port Street, south to St. Ninian's ($1\frac{1}{2}$ miles), then A80, by-passing Denny ($5\frac{1}{2}$ miles), to Castlecary ($3\frac{1}{2}$ miles).

St. Ninian's. To the east, on the then marshy levels of the Forth, was fought the Battle of Bannockburn (1314), in which the Scots, under the redoubtable Robert Bruce, defeated the numerically superior army of Edward II, and the independence of Scotland was secured. Beside the Glasgow road, $\frac{1}{2}$-mile south of the road junction, is a fine Information Centre (1967) of the National Trust for Scotland, and behind this, on the Borestone Brae, where the Scottish king is believed to have raised his standard, are a memorial Rotunda (1964) and a fine equestrian statue of the king, by C. d'O. P. Jackson.

A80 on to the Cumbernauld roundabout ($1\frac{1}{2}$ miles) and thence via Stepps to Alexandra Park (12 miles); then A8 (right) to reach the centre of Glasgow (Buchanan Street; $2\frac{1}{2}$ miles) via Stirling Road and Cathedral Street.

Cumbernauld, to the left of the roundabout, on A73, is a New Town, designated in 1956, with many interesting features. The town centre, in a prominent position on a hill top, was begun in 1966.

6. The Trossachs, Strathearn and Perth

This tour, likewise starting from Glasgow (see Tour 4), runs through charming scenery in the neighbourhood of The Trossachs and the chain of lakes stretching from Loch Katrine by Loch Achray to Loch Venachar, and also takes in Balquhidder, famous for its associations with Rob Roy. Other beautiful lakes are Loch Lubnaig and Loch Earn, from which the lovely vale of Strathearn extends past Comrie to the favourite tourist resort of Crieff. The route goes on past the old castle of Huntingtower to the 'Fair City' of Perth, from which it returns over the Ochil Hills and through Kinross, on the shores of Loch Leven, now a wildlife sanctuary. Crossing the Forth at Kincardine, the road skirts the Campsie Fells on its way back to the commercial and manufacturing centre of Scotland.

From Glasgow (Buchanan Street) by Cowcaddens Street, Garscube Road and A81 for 5 miles, then A809 through the suburb of Bearsden (1 mile) and on to Auchineden (6 miles) and thence to Drymen (6 miles).

The Queen's View, near the road east of Auchineden Hill, affords a distant prospect of Loch Lomond and the serried peaks of the Central Highlands. Drymen is an attractive village from which B837, a tree-shaded road, runs to Balmaha, 4 miles west on the verdant shore of Loch Lomond, with a steamer pier (compare Tour 5).

A811 on to Ballat cross-roads (3½ miles), then A81 (left) for 6½ miles, and A821 (left again) to Aberfoyle (1 mile).

Aberfoyle is a suburbanised village in a beautiful position below the end of the Menteith Hills, on the Highland Fault, which marks the geological division between the Highlands and the Lowlands. The plough coulter hanging from a tree opposite the Bailie Nicol Jarvie Hotel recalls a famous episode in Scott's *Rob Roy*. The road (B829) going on from Aberfoyle leads past Loch Ard, on the north side of the Queen Elizabeth Forest Park, to the isthmus between Loch Katrine and Inversnaid on Loch Lomond (see Tour 4, page 28).

A821 north, climbing steeply across a range of hills, with charming views, then descending to the west end of Loch Achray, from which a road runs west through The Trossachs to the foot of Loch Katrine (5½ miles).

The Trossachs, among the most beautiful parts of Scotland (but greatly over-crowded in the height of summer), are a restricted gorge strewn with rocks and filled with a luxuriant growth of varied trees and plants. They extend from the small but lovely Loch Achray to the pier at the east end of Loch Katrine (steamer cruises in summer), an enchanting lake first made famous by Scott's

Tour 6
154 miles

▷N

Unclassified Roads

Loch Leven

Bridge of Earn
Aberargie
Glenfarg
A90
Perth
A90
Huntingtower
Methven
A85
Milnathort
Crook of Devon
Kinross
A977
Powmill
Forest Mill
Rumbling Bridge
Kincardine
A876
Gilmerton
Crieff
Fowlis Wester
A85
A977
Larbert
Dennyloanhead
Comrie
A803
A80
St. Fillans
Banknock
A85
Loch Earn
Kilsyth
Kirkintilloch
A803
Bishopbriggs
Kingshouse Inn
Strathyre
Pass of Leny
Callander
Campsie Fells
Lochearnhead
A84
A81
Balquhidder
Loch Lubnaig
Brig o' Turk
A821
Loch Venachar
Bearsden
A81
Loch Voil
A821
Aberfoyle
A809
Auchineden
Loch Achray
A811
Loch Katrine
The Trossachs
Drymen
Loch Earn
A85
A84

romantic poem, *The Lady of the Lake*. A footway on the north side affords a delightful view of the rugged Ben Venue, and of Ben Lomond and the peaks beyond Loch Lomond.

A821 on the north side of Loch Achray to Brig o' Turk (2 miles), and thence along the shore of Loch Venachar (beyond which, in 4½ miles, A892 branches right for Callender, on Tour 2).

Brig o' Turk is a hamlet between the two lochs, at the foot of Glen Finglas. Loch Venachar is beautifully situated between the Menteith Hills and the pyramid-shaped Ben Ledi.

A821 on from the road junction for 1 mile, then A84 (left) through the Pass of Leny to the foot of Loch Lubnaig (2 miles), whose east shore it follows nearly to Strathyre (5 miles).

The Pass of Leny is a constricted and wood-filled passage forced by the Leny between the slopes of Ben Ledi and Ben Vorlich. Loch Lubnaig is a sombre lake 4 miles long, hemmed in by steep hillsides clothed in dark woods. Strathyre, to the north, is a small village and angling resort in the deep glen of the same name.

A84 on to the Kingshouse Inn (2 miles) and thence to Lochearnhead (3 miles).

Balquhidder, 2 miles west of the Kingshouse Inn on a by-road, is a pleasant village at the head of Strathyre and the foot of Loch Voil. Robert MacGregor, the notorious freebooter made famous by Scott's *Rob Roy*, is almost certainly buried in the churchyard, but the three tombstones in front of the ruined Old Church (1631), claimed to be those of Rob Roy, his wife and two of his sons, date from long before his time. The road goes on along the north shore of the charming Loch Voil, above which rise the Braes of Balquhidder, in the heart of the MacGregor country, to Inverlochlarig (6 miles), on the site of the house in which Rob Roy died in 1734. Lochearnhead is a village and favourite water-sports resort, facing down the steep-sided loch, above which Ben Vorlich rises proudly to the south.

A85 along the north shore of Loch Earn to St. Fillans (6½ miles).

St. Fillans is a delightful village and a sailing centre at the foot of the loch, from which the river Earn emerges.

A85 on through Strathearn to Comrie (5½ miles).

Comrie is a small town and summer resort finely situated on the strath of the Earn, at the junction with Glen Artney (to the south) and Glen Lednock. A shady path ascends the Lednock for ¾-mile to the De'il's Cauldron, a rock chasm through which the river forces its way.

A85 on through the beautiful strath of the Earn to Crieff (6½ miles).

Crieff is described in Tour 5 (page 32).

A85 on to Gilmerton (2 miles) and thence, passing south of Fowlis Wester (3 miles), to Methven (6 miles).

Fowlis Wester is an attractive village on a hill, with a restored 13th century church. Methven is a large village in the churchyard of which are remains of a 15th century collegiate church, now the burial-place of the Methven family. Margaret Tudor, the Queen of James IV, died in 1541 at Methven Castle, 1 mile east, a large house mostly rebuilt in the 17th century.

A85 on to Huntingtower (4 miles).

Huntingtower, on a bank south of the Almond, has a Castle (admission 10 to 7; October-March to 4; Sundays from 2) consisting of two large 15th-16th century towers, over 9 feet apart, connected by a late-17th century addition. The great hall has a wooden ceiling of about 1540 with perhaps the earliest tempera paintings in Scotland. The castle is famous for an episode known as the 'Raid of Ruthven,' in which James VI, at the age of 16, was held here by the Earl of Gowrie and other conspirators.

A85 on, to join A9 before entering Perth (2½ miles) by Dunkeld Road.

Perth, often called the 'Fair City,' is an old Royal Burgh and a historic county town and thriving agricultural centre, enclosed by delightfully wooded hills. The capital of Scotland from its foundation in 1210 by William the Lion until the 15th century, it is well situated between the large meadows of the North and South Inch, on the broad Tay, which is crossed by an 18th century bridge by John Smeaton. The Art Gallery and Museum (admission 10 to 1 and 2 to 5; Tuesdays and Fridays also 6 to 8; Sundays 2 to 4), in George Street, has good collections illustrating the history and natural history of Perthshire. Near by is the Fair Maid's House, said to be that described in Scott's novel, *The Fair Maid of Perth.* St. John's Church (admission Monday-Friday 11 to 1 and 2 to 4, Saturdays 10 to 12 and 2 to 4) is a fine Gothic building of the 15th century. Here in 1559 John Knox preached his famous iconoclastic sermon that urged " the purging of the churches from idolatry."

A90 south, leaving Perth by Edinburgh Road and crossing the ridge of Moncreiffe Hill to Bridge of Earn (3½ miles), and thence across a plain to Aberargie (3 miles); then up Glen Farg to the village of Glenfarg (4½ miles).

Bridge of Earn is a small summer resort and angling centre on the Earn, near the east end of its wide strath. Glenfarg is at the head of a delightful ravine in the northern slopes of the Ochil Hills.

A90 on to Milnathort (4½ miles).

Milnathort is a small agricultural town to the north-west of Loch Leven. Burleigh Castle (key at the farm opposite), ½-mile east, is a fine 16th century tower-house of the Balfours.

A90 on to Kinross.

Kinross is a quiet county town and a favourite angling resort on the west side of the loch, most of the shores of which are now a

38

nature reserve. On a peninsula is Kinross House, built for himself about 1685 by Sir William Bruce, who introduced classical architecture into Scotland, and on an island (reached by ferry boat). ¼-mile offshore, is Lochleven Castle, famous for the escape from imprisonment here in 1568 of Mary, Queen of Scots.

A977 west to Crook of Devon (5½ miles) and thence to Rumbling Bridge (1½ miles).

Crook of Devon is a village named from its position on a sharp bend of the river Devon. At Rumbling Bridge, ¼-mile to the right of the road, the river pushes through a deep and narrow ravine, with charming cascades.

A977 on to Powmill (1 mile) and thence (right) to Forest Mill (5 miles) and on to Kincardine (5 miles).

Kincardine is a small town on the Forth, which is crossed by a bridge built in 1936, with a central swing span of 100 yards.

A876 across the river and on, passing north of Stenhousemuir and Larbert, and crossing A9 (6½ miles) and the river Carron, to Dennyloanhead (3½ miles); then A80 (the main Glasgow road, see Tour 5) to Banknock (1½ miles) and A803 (right) to Kilsyth (4½ miles).

Kilsyth is a mining and quarrying town with other industries, below the grass and bracken covered Kilsyth Hills, which rise to 1,870 feet. To the south, beyond the river Kelvin, is a lower range of wooded hills with traces of the Antonine Wall (see Tour 1, page 10).

A803 on to Kirkintilloch (5 miles) and thence via Bishopbriggs (4 miles) to reach the centre of Glasgow (Buchanan Street; 4 miles) via Springburn Road, Castle Street and Parliamentary Road.

Kirkintilloch is an old-established burgh, partly residential and partly industrial, with iron foundries and other works (but no public houses), in the Kelvin Valley. In Peel Park are the earthworks of a Roman fort that stood on the Antonine Wall.

Tour 7
148 miles

Dunstaffnage Castle

Auchnacloich

Loch Etive

Connel
A85

Bonawe
Bridge of Awe

Kerrera

Oban
A85

Taynuilt

Lochawe
A85

A816

Cleigh

Pass of Brander

Daln

Loch Feochan

A819

Seil

Kilninver

Loch Awe

Cladich

B844

Loch Melfort

A819

Kilmelford

Glen Aray

A816

B840

Inveraray
A83

Auchindrain

Loch Craignish

Carnassarie Castle

Furnace

Kilmartin

Crarae

Loch Crinan

Crinan

Dunadd

A816

Lochgair

Cairnbaan
A817
A83

A83

Lochgilphead

Ardrishaig

B8024

Loch Fyne

Achahoish

Loch Coalisport

Knapdale

A83

Tarbert

B8024

Kilberry

Dunmore

West Loch Tarbert

△
N

|||||||||||||||||||||
Unclassified Road

Kintyre

7. Loch Etive and Loch Awe, Loch Fyne and the West Coast

This tour and the next start at Oban, a busy fishing town and a favourite summer resort with numerous steamer services, on the west coast of Argyll. The road skirts the fine sea-loch of Loch Etive and goes through the dramatic Pass of Brander to the beautiful inland lake of Loch Awe. The tour also includes the delightful town of Inveraray, with its majestic baronial castle of the Campbell chiefs, as well as the new village-museum at Auchindrain, to the south, and the small burgh of Lochgilphead, on an inlet of the extensive Loch Fyne. The route makes a circuit over part of the long peninsula of Knapdale and Kintyre, from which the return road to Oban takes in Kilmartin, the centre of a region remarkable for its prehistoric remains, and touches many sea lochs with views of the Inner Hebridean islands, including Jura and Mull.

Oban is a thriving fishing port and market town, and a popular holiday and yachting resort, on the shores and slopes of a sheltered bay almost landlocked by the island of Kerrera, and renowned for its views across the Firth of Lorn to the mountains of Mull (best at sunset). Its growth coincided with the development of the tourist industry in the Western Highlands in the 19th century, and the town is consequently mainly of modern aspect. The Railway Quay, on the south side of Oban Bay, is usually busy with steamers and fishing boats. From the North Pier, overlooking the Inner Harbour, the bay is skirted by the Corran Esplanade (with a concert pavilion), leading to the distinctive white Christ Church (1957) and the granite Roman Catholic Cathedral (by Sir Giles G. Scott, 1932) of the diocese of Argyll and the Isles. Farther on is the ruined medieval tower of Dunollie Castle, the stronghold of the MacDougalls, Lords of Lorn, and the shore road ends at Ganavan, a favourite bathing place on a fine sandy bay. On the hill behind the town is the prominent but unfinished McCaig Tower, a circular structure begun about 1890, commanding a wonderful view over the firth to Mull and the peninsula of Morven. Steamers ply round the island of Mull in summer, calling at Iona and Staffa (weather permitting) and at Tobermory, the capital of Mull.

From Oban by A85, passing south of Dunstaffnage Castle (2½ miles) and reaching the south shore of Loch Etive near Connel (2 miles).

Dunstaffnage Castle, on a promontory facing the entrance into the loch, belonged to the MacDougalls of Lorn, but was taken by Robert Bruce after his victory in the Pass of Brander (see below) and became a royal fortress. The ruins (under restoration in 1968) consist of a tall rectangular structure with a gatehouse, possibly of the 13th century, and a 15th century extension with walls 10 feet thick. Flora Macdonald, who helped Prince Charles Edward to

41

escape in 1746, was held prisoner here for several weeks. The early-medieval chapel near by is the burial-place of the Campbells of Dunstaffnage. Loch Etive is a sea-loch about 18 miles long, opening east of Firth of Lorn, and enclosed by fine mountains. At Connel, a narrow reach near its mouth is crossed by a large cantilever bridge (see Tour 8).

A85 on, passing a side-road to Auchnacloich (3 miles), and thence to Taynuilt (4 miles).

Auchnacloich is on the south shore of Loch Etive, and from it a motor launch plies up the loch in summer to Lochetivehead. Taynuilt is a scattered but attractive village near the foot of the wooded Glen Nant. Bonawe, 1 mile north, where the river Awe enters Loch Etive, affords a fine view up the loch.

A85 on to the Bridge of Awe (3 miles) and thence through the Pass of Brander and along the north shore of Loch Awe to the village of Lochawe (6 miles).

Loch Awe. Near the Bridge of Awe, in 1308, Robert Bruce trapped and almost destroyed the warlike MacDougalls. The Pass of Brander is a savage rock-strewn defile below the sheer precipices of Ben Cruachan (3,689 feet). Into its east end projects the long narrow north-west arm of Loch Awe, one of the largest lochs in Scotland (some 24 miles long) and one of the most delightful. Its head is at the south-west end, from which it originally drained into the sea at Loch Crinan (see below); its waters are now carried away through the pass to Loch Etive. Before reaching the modern village of Lochawe the road passes St. Conan's Kirk, an elaborate church mostly in the Romanesque style, built in 1907-30. The terrace below allows a charming view over the loch, with Ben Lui rising to the east. Kilchurn Castle, on a peninsula extending into the north-east arm of the loch, and reached from Lochawe by boat, is a ruined 15th century keep of the Campbells of Glenorchy, with 17th century additions.

A85 on round Loch Awe for 1½ miles, then A819 along the east shore of the loch to Cladich (5½ miles). (A85 goes on to Dalmally, on Tour 4.) The road affords a grand view of Kilchurn Castle and the magnificent slopes of Ben Cruachan rising from the opposite shore of the loch. A819 south, ascending away from Loch Awe, then from the summit (675 feet) descending through the beautiful woods of Glen Aray to Inveraray (9½ miles).

Inveraray, on the west shore of Loch Fyne, near the mouth of the charming Glen Shira, is a small but historic royal burgh laid out on a new site after 1743 and largely and successfully rebuilt in 1957-61 for the Ministry of Works. At the north end of the main street is a fine Celtic cross brought from Iona, and at the other end is the classical Church (1794), divided into two identical parts for services in English and Gaelic. The Courthouse (1820), to the east, is now a centre for training young people in Highland crafts.

Crombie's Land, a white house facing the loch, was the birthplace of Neil Munro, who laid scenes in *John Splendid* and *The New Road* in the town. Inveraray Castle (admission Easter to mid-October, daily, except Sunday mornings, 10 to 12.30 and 2 to 6; closed Fridays until the end of June), in a large park near the foot of Glen Aray, is the seat of the Duke of Argyll, the Highlanders' MacCailean Mòr, or MacCallum More, the head of the Clan Campbell. The imposing Scottish baronial mansion, rebuilt in the 18th century, with massive round towers at the corners and a square central tower, has a finely decorated interior containing family portraits by Gainsborough, Ramsay and Raeburn, and historical relics (of Rob Roy and others).

A83 south, on the west side of Loch Fyne, to Auchindrain ($5\frac{1}{2}$ miles) and thence to Furnace ($2\frac{1}{2}$ miles).

Loch Fyne, 42 miles long, is one of the largest sea-lochs in Scotland, and has long been famous for its herrings. At Auchindrain, the whole clachan or hamlet was converted in 1967 into a Museum of Farming Life (admission weekdays, 11 to 5), the first folk museum in Scotland to utilise original buildings on their sites and to illustrate multiple-tenancy farming, in which the families worked the land as a community. Furnace is named from a now-abandoned smelting-mill.

A83 on to Crarae (2 miles) and Lochgair (7 miles), and thence to Lochgilphead ($7\frac{1}{2}$ miles), where the direct road to Oban (A816; see below) branches right.

Crarae is a hamlet with the lovely Gardens (admission April-October, daily, until dusk) of Crarae Lodge, noted for their rare trees and shrubs. Lochgair is a hamlet on a small sandy inlet of Loch Fyne, in charmingly wooded country. Lochgilphead, the county town of Argyll, is a pleasant small market town at the head of a larger inlet. Kilmory Castle, above the east shore of Loch Gilp, is a large house of about 1750.

A83 on, west of Loch Gilp, to Ardrishaig ($2\frac{1}{2}$ miles) and thence along the west shore of Loch Fyne, in the district of Knapdale, to Tarbert (11 miles).

Ardrishaig is a village at the entrance to the Crinan Canal, cut in 1793-1801 to Crinan (see below) to avoid the long and sometimes stormy voyage round the Mull of Kintyre, to the south. Tarbert is a village and small summer resort with good sands on the shore of East Loch Tarbert, a small inlet on the west of Loch Fyne, near its mouth, and the chief centre of the herring fishery. The ruined 14th century Castle was a stronghold of Robert Bruce and later of James II.

A83 on across an isthmus only 1 mile wide to West Loch Tarbert, then by an unclassified road (right) skirting the loch head to reach B8024, which runs through woods on the north side of the loch to Dunmore (7 miles from Tarbert).

West Loch Tarbert is a beautiful sea-loch 10 miles long that extends from the north end of the Sound of Gigha and separates the peninsula of Knapdale, on the north, from that of Kintyre.

B8024 on across the south tip of Knapdale to Kilberry (7 miles), on the west coast, and north along the shore of Loch Coalisport to Achahoish (10 miles), then across the ridge of Knapdale, reaching a height of 634 feet, to rejoin A83 for Ardrishaig ($7\frac{1}{2}$ miles). The road along the west coast affords splendid views over the sea to the islands of Islay and Jura, with the distinctive peaks of the Paps of Jura.

Loch Coalisport or Killisport is a fine sea-loch 6 miles long, with well-wooded shores.

A83 on to the head of Loch Gilp (2 miles), then A817 on for $\frac{1}{2}$-mile to join A816 (see above) which goes on to Cairnbaan (7 miles from Ardrishaig). From Ardrishaig (see above) the road follows the Crinan Canal, which turns west from Cairnbaan, following B841 to its exit in Loch Crinan ($4\frac{1}{2}$ miles).

Loch Crinan is a large inlet east of the Sound of Jura. The 13th century Duntroon Castle, on its north shore, was a Campbell stronghold until 1792.

A816 on to Dunadd ($2\frac{1}{2}$ miles).

Dunadd, left of the road, is a curious isolated hill, once an islet in an estuary, crowned by a hill-fort identified as the 'capital' of Dalriada, the early kingdom of the Scots. On the rocky top are an incised boat-sculpture, a fine carving of a boar, and a footprint, said to be the place of inauguration of the kings. The wide view over the reclaimed marshland includes Loch Linnhe and the Paps of Jura.

A816 on to Kilmartin (3 miles).

Kilmartin, in a district notable for its prehistoric remains, is an attractive village in a tributary valley of the Add. In the church-yard are a great number of sculptured stones, including two fine crosses and over 30 gravestones, some of them carved with figures of knights.

A816 on to Carnassarie Castle ($1\frac{1}{2}$ miles) and thence, skirting the head of Loch Craignish and the south shore of Loch Melfort, to Kilmelford ($12\frac{1}{2}$ miles).

Carnassarie Castle is a ruined 16th century tower-house built by the first Protestant Bishop of the Isles. The road opposite (B840) leads to Ford (3 miles), a village at the delightful upper end of Loch Awe (see above). Kilmelford is a small village and angling resort near the head of Loch Melfort, an attractive loch whose sea-ward end is sheltered by the island of Luing.

A816 on through the Pass of Melfort and thence to Kilninver ($6\frac{1}{2}$ miles), near the south shore of Loch Feochan, then round the head of the loch to Cleigh (5 miles) and on to Oban (4 miles).

Loch Feochan is a narrow loch, $4\frac{1}{2}$ miles long, opening off the Firth of Lorn, opposite Mull. From Kilninver, B844 runs south-west, crossing the Clachan Sound, an arm of the sea, by a hump-backed bridge, to the island of Seil, noted for its slate quarries.

Fort William

A82

North Ballachulish

Loch Leven

Ballachulish Ferry

Glencoe

Altnafeadh

Kingshous Hotel

South Ballachulish

A82

Glen Coe

Ranno Moc

Loch Linnhe

A328

Duror

Portnacroish

A828

Glasdrum

Loch Tulla

A82

Appin

Port Appin

Loch Creran

Inveroran

Bridge Orchy

Lismore Island

A828

New Selma

Loch Etive

Dunstaffnage Castle

Tynd

Bonawe

A85

Lochawe

Kerrera

Connel

A85

A85

Crianlarich

A85

Oban

Taynuilt

Dalmally

Pass of Brander

G Fal

Cladich

Loch Awe

A819

Ardlui

Dundarave Castle

A83

Inveruglas

Glen Aray

A83

Cairndow

Inveraray

A82

Rest & Be Thankful

A83

Glen Croe

Ta

Ardgartan

Arrochar

Loch Long

Lo Lom

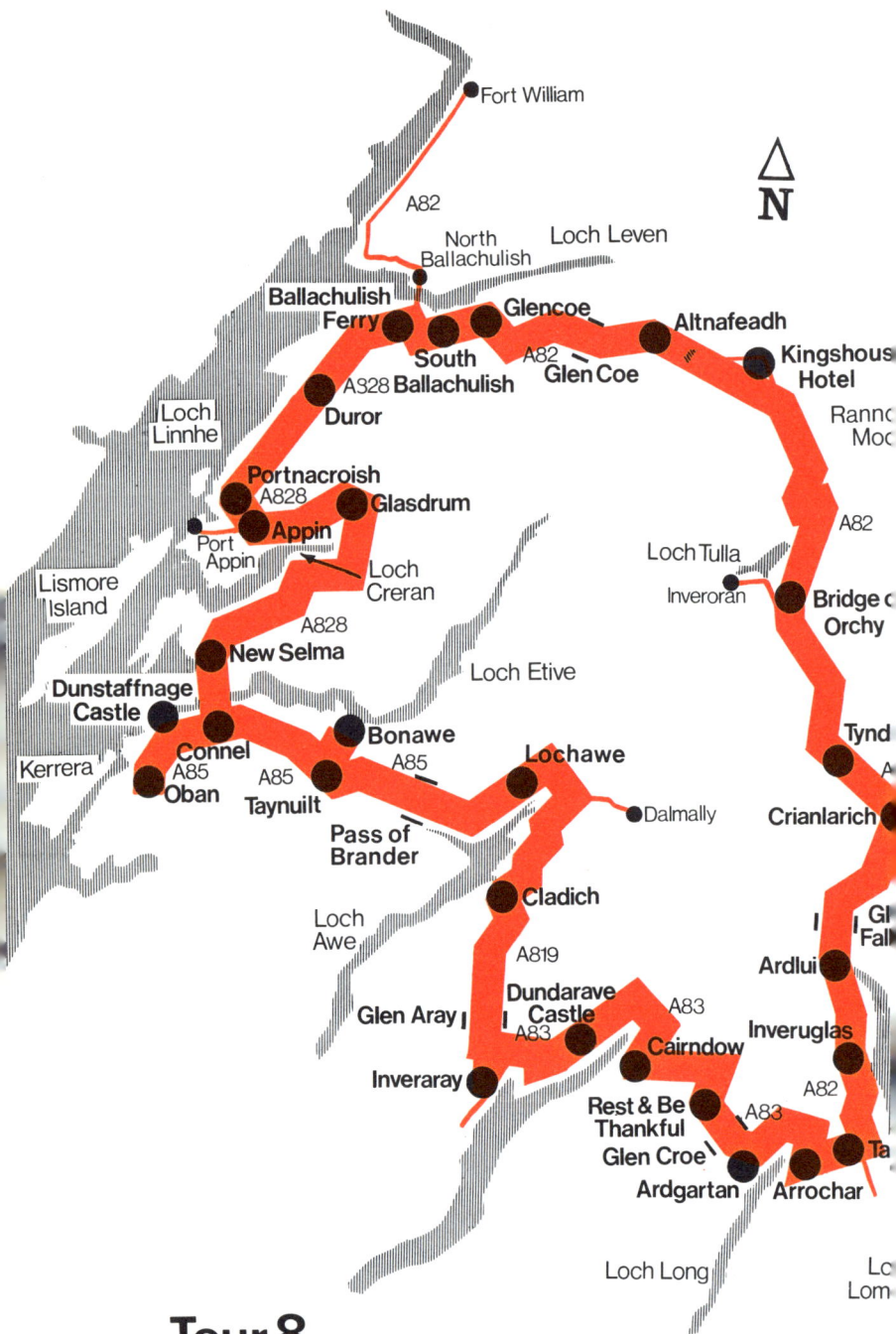

Tour 8
151miles

N

8. Glen Coe and Rannoch Moor, Loch Lomond and Loch Fyne

This tour, like Tour 7, starts at Oban, and it takes in no less than seven major lochs, the inland lakes of Loch Lomond and Loch Awe, and the fjords of Loch Etive, Loch Creran, Loch Leven, Loch Long and Loch Fyne. The most magnificent scenery, however, is in the great gorge of Glen Coe, to which the bleak moorland wastes of Rannoch Moor form a striking contrast, as do the bulky mountains around Strath Fillan. The tour also includes the charming district of Appin, bordering the coast of Loch Linnhe, the popular summer resort of Arrochar, with its splendid view of the Ben Arthur range of mountains, and the interesting town and imposing castle of Inveraray.

Oban is described in Tour 7 (page 41).

From Oban via A85 to Connel ($4\frac{1}{2}$ miles). A828 north across Loch Etive by the Connel Bridge and through the district of Benderloch to New Selma ($2\frac{1}{2}$ miles).

Benderloch, the hilly peninsula between Loch Etive and Loch Creran, ends on the west in a hammerhead-shaped promontory, the south part of which encloses Ardmucknish Bay, with wooded shores.

A828 on, passing the road to Barcaldine Castle ($1\frac{1}{2}$ miles), then along the south shore of Loch Creran to its head at Glasdrum ($8\frac{1}{2}$ miles).

Barcaldine Castle is a restored 15th century house near the south shore of Loch Creran, a beautiful sea-loch about $8\frac{1}{2}$ miles long, with fine wooded shores, opening from the Lynn of Lorn, the channel between Lismore Island and the mainland. Glasdrum is at the foot of the richly-wooded Glen Creran.

A828 on, returning along the north shore of Loch Creran and traversing the Strath of Appin to Appin (5 miles).

Appin is a hamlet in the mountainous district of the same name, long the terrain of the Stewarts. A by-road runs west to Port Appin ($2\frac{1}{2}$ miles), a remote village on the east shore of Loch Linnhe, opposite the north end of the long island of Lismore.

A828 on to Portnacroish (1 mile) and thence along the shore of Loch Linnhe to Duror ($5\frac{1}{2}$ miles).

Portnacroish is a village on Loch Laich, a small inlet of Loch Linnhe. On an islet offshore is Castle Stalker, long the stronghold of the Stewarts of Appin, built about 1500 for a visit of James IV and recently restored. The coast road to Duror commands splendid views over the loch to the mountains of Morvern and Ardgour. Beyond the scattered village is the hilly promontory of Ardsheal, where Colin Campbell of Glenure, the 'Red Fox', was shot in

1752 by an unknown assassin, though James Stewart 'of the Glens' was found guilty (by a jury of Campbells) and hanged for the murder. The 'Appin Murder' forms the central theme of Stevenson's *Kidnapped* and *Catriona*.

A828 on to Ballachulish Ferry (6 miles).

Ballachulish Ferry is on the south shore of Loch Leven, a fine sea-loch about 11 miles long, opening off the east side of Loch Linnhe. A car ferry (frequent service daily; no reservations necessary) crosses the narrowest section of the loch to North Ballachulish ($\frac{1}{2}$ mile), reached also by road via Kinlochleven.

A828 on beside Loch Leven to South Ballachulish (2 miles), and thence to the village of Glencoe ($1\frac{1}{2}$ miles).

South Ballachulish is a quarrying village producing large roofing slates. Glencoe, as it is usually called (though properly named Carnoch), is a relatively modern village at the foot of Glen Coe, dominated by the conical Pap of Glencoe. At the east end, on the site of the old clachan, is a monument commemorating the Massacre of Glencoe (1692), one of the most infamous episodes in Scottish history, when some 40 of the Macdonalds, whose chief had failed to take the oath of allegiance to William III in time, were assassinated by royal troops under the command of Robert Campbell of Glenlyon.

[A82 goes on along the south shore of Loch Leven to Kinlochleven (7 miles), a small town with aluminium works, then returns by the north shore (with a fine view of Glen Coe) to North Ballachulish (9 miles).] The tour climbs by A82 south-east up Glen Coe, the most famous of all the Highland glens, and out to Altnafeadh ($9\frac{1}{2}$ miles), and goes on thence across a moor towards the Kingshouse Hotel ($2\frac{1}{2}$ miles).

Glen Coe is a deep and rugged ravine hemmed in by towering mountains. The lower section, as far as the Clachaig Inn (on the east side), is remarkably verdant, but as the road crosses the Coe to the shallow Loch Achtriochtan, the glen changes its character to one of magnificent austerity. On the north, Aonach Eagach presents a solid wall of rock, and to the south rise the 'Three Sisters of Glen Coe', with huge precipitous crags, the northern buttresses of three ridges extending from the massive Bidean nam Bian. Above the road, 2 miles east of the loch, is The Study, or 'Stiddie' (i.e. 'anvil'), a rock platform which commands the finest view. The Kingshouse Hotel, to the left of the road, is an old-established hostelry in the centre of a favourite winter-sports region.

A82 across Rannoch Moor, descending thence to the east end of Loch Tulla ($9\frac{1}{2}$ miles), and on to Bridge of Orchy (3 miles).

Rannoch Moor is the largest and most desolate moor in the Central Highlands, a vast region of bog and heather, interspersed with many small lakes. Loch Tulla is an upland lake, $2\frac{1}{4}$ miles long, below the moorland heights of the Black Mount, a noted deer forest. Achallader Castle, to the east, is a ruined stronghold of the Campbells of Glenlyon where the massacre is said to have been planned. Bridge of Orchy is a small angling resort on the Orchy near the head of its glen. A8005, part of the old road to Glen Coe, runs north-west to Inveroran, a solitary retreat near the west end of Loch Tulla.

A82 across the watershed of the Grampian Mountains to Tyndrum (6½ miles).

Tyndrum is an angling resort well situated at the head of Strath Fillan, surrounded by grand mountains, and at the junction of the direct road from Oban via Dalmally (see Tour 4, page 28).

A82 down Strath Fillan to Crianlarich (5 miles) then over the watershed and down Glen Falloch to Ardlui (8 miles), at the head of Loch Lomond.

Crianlarich is a village and railway centre in an open moorland setting, at the lower end of the strath. Ardlui, at the foot of the tree-filled Glen Falloch, is surrounded by fine mountains that include Ben Vorlich and Beinn a' Choin. Loch Lomond, nearly 22 miles long, is the largest inland lake in Britain and one of the most beautiful, with steep shores enclosing its narrow upper reach.

A82 down the west shore of the loch to Inveruglas (5 miles) and thence to Tarbet (3 miles).

Inveruglas, which has a power station fed by the waters of Loch Sloy, behind Ben Vorlich, is connected by a passenger ferry with Inversnaid, in the 'Rob Roy' country on the opposite shore. Tarbet is a hamlet with a pier called at by the steamers which ply on Loch Lomond in summer. The charmingly wooded shores are dominated by the graceful peak of Ben Lomond, rising on the east side of the water.

A83 west, across the narrow isthmus separating the loch from Loch Long, to Arrochar (1½ miles), and thence, round the head of the loch, crossing the foot of Glen Loin, to Ardgartan (2½ miles).

Arrochar is a village and popular holiday resort beautifully situated near the head of Loch Long, with a wonderful view of the forked peak of Ben Arthur, usually called the Cobbler. Ardgartan, at the mouth of the Croe in the loch, has a large camping ground in Ardgartan Forest, part of the Argyll National Forest Park.

A83 on, ascending Glen Croe to Rest and be Thankful (4½ miles).

Glen Croe, once wild and desolate, is now partly afforested. The road through it ascends steadily across the south side of Ben Arthur, above the old road, which keeps mainly to the valley bottom, then climbs from its head in steep zigzags to the summit of the pass (860 feet) near a stone seat inscribed 'Rest and be Thankful', from which there is an impressive view.

A83 on, down Glen Kinglas to Cairndow (5 miles), on the shore of Loch Fyne, then round the head of the loch to Dundarave Castle (5½ miles).

Loch Fyne is described in Tour 7 (page 43). Dundarave Castle, on the upper reach, is a restored 16th century tower-house of the Macnachtons, the ' Doom Castle ' of Neil Munro's novel.

A83 on, along the loch shore, to Inveraray (5 miles).

Inveraray is described in Tour 7 (page 42).

A819 north up Glen Aray, then from the road summit down to Cladich (9½ miles) and along the shore of Loch Awe to its north-east end (5½ miles), 1 mile short of Dalmally (Tour 4). A85 (left) beside the north shore of the loch, via Lochawe village, and through the Pass of Brander to Taynuilt (10½ miles), then on via Connel to Oban (11½ miles).

All the places between Inveraray and Connel are described in Tour 7 (page 42).

9. The Great Glen, Inverness and Strath Spey

This tour, starting from the favourite tourist centre of Fort William, with its thriving new industries, traverses the Great Glen, which runs right across country to Inverness, a focal point of northern Scotland, and divides the Central Highlands from the Northern and Western Highlands. The route takes in the delightful inland lakes of Loch Ness and Loch Laggan, the unique ' Parallel Roads ' in Glen Roy and the site of the disastrous battle of Culloden, the grave of the second Jacobite rising, and it affords wonderful prospects of the great Cairngorm massif. Its many points of varied interest include the old fortress of Urquhart Castle overlooking Loch Ness, the new abbey of Fort Augustus, the episcopal cathedral at Inverness, the excellent Holiday Centre at Aviemore and, not least, the absorbing museums of Highland life at Fort William, Inverness and Kingussie.

Fort William, near the head of Loch Linnhe, where it turns west towards Loch Eil, is a busy town and a popular tourist and sailing centre, the usual starting point for the ascent of Ben Nevis. The 17th century fort, rebuilt for William III, after whom it is named, with the object of quelling the rebellious Highlanders, was pulled down in 1890 to make way for the West Highland Railway. The town, mostly developed since the opening of the railway in 1894, has been given a new lease of life by the large industries established in the neighbourhood. In Cameron Square is the interesting West Highland Museum (admission weekdays, 9.30 to 5, June-August to 9), containing old ' bygones ', farm implements and domestic utensils, collections illustrating local geology and industry and tartan weaving, and Jacobite relics. Cow Hill, to the south-east of the town, affords a fine view of the beautiful Glen Nevis, with the slopes of Ben Nevis (4,418 feet), the highest mountain in Britain, rising above it.

From Fort William by A82 northward to Inverlochy ($1\frac{1}{2}$ miles).

Inverlochy, at the mouth of the Lochy in Loch Linnhe, and now practically a suburb of Fort William, has huge aluminium works, connected with Loch Treig, 15 miles away, by a pipe-line through Ben Nevis. The ruined old Inverlochy Castle is a large square fortress, probably of the late-15th century. The 19th century Castle, over 1 mile farther on, is now the centre of an extensive cattle ranch. The road beyond it affords a splendid view of the stark precipices on the north face of Ben Nevis, with deep gullies where snow lingers all the year round.

A82 on to Spean Bridge (8 miles).

Spean Bridge is a village on a fine reach of the Spean, at the foot of its glen (see page 56). Beyond it, the Inverness road passes the Commando Memorial (1951), effectively placed, looking out over the rugged country (where the commandos trained during the Second World War) soaring up to the great mass of Ben Nevis.

Tour 9
162 miles

N △

Unclassified Road

Culloden Moor
Inverness
Beauly Firth
B851
Loch Moy
Daviot
A9
B9006
A9
Tomatin
Slochd Summit
Carrbridge
A9
Aviemore
Alvie
Loch Insh
Kincraig
A9
Kingussie
Cluny Castle
Newtonmore
A86
Laggan
Drumgask
Loch Laggan
Kinloch Laggan
A86
Loch Moy
Moy Lodge
Roybridge
A86
Spean Bridge
A82
A82
A86
Invergarry
Loch Lochy
Laggan Locks
Loch Oich
Fort Augustus
Invermoriston
A82
Loch Ness
Urquhart Castle
Drumnadrochit
A82

A82 on to Loch Lochy (5 miles) and along its south-east shore for Laggan Locks (7 miles), and thence, skirting Loch Oich, to Invergarry (3 miles).

Glen More, or the Great Glen, which the road enters, is a trench-like ravine which runs right across Scotland to Inverness. Loch Lochy is a narrow loch nearly 10 miles long, with steep shores mostly covered by woods. At Laggan Locks the road crosses the Caledonian Canal, opened in 1822 and enlarged in 1847, traversing the Great Glen between Loch Linnhe and the Beauly Firth, a distance of over 60 miles, and taking in the lochs of Lochy, Oich and Ness. Invergarry is a village enchantingly placed at the foot of Glen Garry and above the shores of Loch Oich, on a rock near which are the ruins of the Castle, a stronghold of the MacDonells of Glengarry.

A82 on to Fort Augustus (7 miles) and thence along the north-west shore of Loch Ness to Invermoriston (6½ miles).

Fort Augustus is a large village and a tourist resort on the Oich and the Caledonian Canal at their emergence into the head of Loch Ness. The disused remains of the fort, named after William Augustus, Duke of Cumberland, the victor of Culloden (see below), were sold in 1867 to Lord Lovat, who gave the site to the Bene-dictine order. The Abbey established here in 1876 was colonised by monks from the Schottenkloster at Regensburg (Germany), founded in 1074 by a Scottish monk and dissolved in 1862. The tall Romanesque-style church, begun in 1914, still awaits comple-tion. Loch Ness, 23 miles long and over 900 feet deep in places, is one of the longest lakes in Scotland and a major link in the Caledonian Canal scheme. Its shores, enclosed by moorland hills, are now mostly clothed with plantations. The loch, which has never been known to freeze, is now famous for its ' monster ', about which there are many stories, but no conclusive evidence. Invermoriston is a small village exquisitely situated near the foot of the wooded Glen Moriston.

A82 on beside Loch Ness, passing the Cobb Memorial, to Urquhart Castle (10½ miles) and thence to Drumnadrochit (2 miles).

Urquhart Castle (admission 10 to 7; October-March to 4; Sundays from 2), dramatically placed on a bold promontory above the loch, south of Urquhart Bay, is a large and impressive ruin, mostly of the 16th-17th centuries, but incorporating a fortification of the 12th century and later, seized and strengthened in 1296 by Edward I, and given in 1509 by James IV to the Seafield Grants. Beside the shore road over 1 mile south is a memorial to John Cobb, who lost his life on the loch in 1952 while attempting to break the water speed record of 206 m.p.h. Drumnadrochit is a pleasant village in the lower part of Glen Urquhart, which opens to Loch Ness in Urquhart Bay.

A82 on along the shore of Loch Ness to its lower end, then through the valley of the Ness to Inverness (15 miles).

Inverness, a busy tourist and commercial centre and a royal burgh, the 'capital of the Highlands', is mainly of modern aspect, but is well situated on the Ness, $4\frac{1}{2}$ miles below the foot of the loch and about 1 mile from the mouth of the river in the Moray Firth. The large Castle, rebuilt in 1834-46 as the county offices and law courts, replaces the old castle in which Shakespeare laid scenes in *Macbeth*. On the Castle Hill, which affords a charming view up the Ness, is a statue of Flora Macdonald, who assisted Prince Charles Edward in his escape after the disaster of Culloden. The fine Museum and Art Gallery (admission weekdays, 10 to 12.45 and 2.15 to 5.15), built in 1966, has notable Highland collections and Jacobite relics. Old buildings in Inverness include Queen Mary's House, in Bridge Street, where the Queen of Scots lodged when she was refused admission to the castle, and the late-16th century Abertarff House (now the northern headquarters of the Highland Association) and the 17th century Dunbar's Hospital, both in Church Street. In the same churchyard are the High Parish Church and the Greyfriars Free Church (formerly the Old Gaelic Church), both of the late-18th century. On the west bank of the river is the dignified St. Andrew's Cathedral (admission daily, 9 to 9), built in 1869, for the episcopal see of Moray, Ross and Caithness. The Northern Meeting, held near by in September, is noted for its Highland Games and other characteristic Scottish events.

A9, leaving Inverness by High Street and Eastgate, for $2\frac{1}{2}$ miles, then B9006 (left) to Culloden Moor or Muir ($3\frac{1}{2}$ miles), crossing the battlefield.

Culloden Moor, now mostly covered by plantations, was the scene in 1746 of the Battle of Culloden (the last battle fought on British soil), in which the Hanoverian forces under the Duke of Cumberland defeated the Jacobites under 'Bonnie Prince Charlie', and the last hopes of the return of the House of Stuart were crushed. Cairns and stones commemorate the fallen on both sides. Old Leanach farmhouse, said to have been the prince's headquarters, remains as it was in his day (but is now an information centre); the Cumberland Stone, near the cross-roads farther east, is a boulder from which the duke is claimed to have reviewed his troops. The road south, crossing B851, leads to the Clava Cairns ($\frac{3}{4}$ mile), three huge burial cairns of the late-Neolithic or early-Bronze Age, surrounded by circles of standing stones.

B851 (see above) south-west for 4 miles from Culloden Moor, then A9 (left) to Daviot ($\frac{1}{2}$ mile) and on to Loch Moy (5 miles).

Daviot. The road ascending from here affords a splendid retrospect over the Moray and Beauly Firths to the Black Isle and Ben Wyvis and of other peaks of the Highlands to the west. Loch Moy lies on a high moorland, but is surrounded by forest. On an island are the remains of the medieval Castle of the Mackintoshes, whose chief now lives at Moy Hall, rebuilt in 1955, on the shore.

A9 on into Strathdearn at Tomatin (4 miles), then up to Slochd

Summit (3½ miles), before descending at length to Carrbridge (6 miles).

Slochd Summit (1,333 feet) is on a north-east extension of the broad Monadhliath Mountains. From here the road commands a superb prospect of the Cairngorm Mountains ahead, with Cairn Gorm on the left and Braeriach on the right of the deep gash of the Lairig Ghru pass, beyond which is seen Ben Macdhui (4,300 feet), the second highest peak in Britain and the centre of the highest mountain mass. Carrbridge is a village and winter-sports resort on the Dulnain, a tributary of the Spey, with the arch of an 18th century bridge.

A9 on into Strath Spey for Aviemore (7 miles) and thence to Alvie (2½ miles) and on through the strath to Kincraig (3½ miles).

Aviemore is a long, plain village on the Spey in the broad and beautifully-wooded strath, and a popular tourist centre and winter-sports resort, the most convenient base for exploring the Cairn-gorms. Near the station is the successful new Holiday Centre, opened in 1966, the first of its kind in Britain, with hotels and restaurants, a theatre and concert hall, and numerous sporting facilities. To the south-east, beyond the river, extends the delight-ful Rothiemurchus Forest, which preserves many survivors of the once-extensive Caledonian Forest, and encloses the charming small lake of Loch-an-Eilean. Alvie is a hamlet on the little Loch Alvie, which is separated from the river by the wooded Tor of Alvie. Kincraig is a village on the Spey below its outflow from Loch Insh. The parish church of Insh, beyond the river, occupies a site used for Christian worship since the 6th century.

A9 on through the strath to Kingussie (5½ miles).

Kingussie is a small town on the Spey, north of the mountainous district of Badenoch. Near the main street at the east end is the fascinating Highland Folk Museum (admission weekdays, May-September, 10 to 4), which includes an 18th century house contain-ing textiles, domestic utensils, craft work, etc. In the grounds are an old barn, with agricultural implements, and representative build-ings brought from various parts of northern Scotland.

A9 on to Newtonmore (3½ miles).

Newtonmore is a long village in well-wooded country near the head of the strath. Clan Macpherson House (admission weekdays, Easter-September, 10 to 12 and 2 to 6) is now the interesting small museum of the clan.

A86 on through the upper valley of the Spey to Cluny Castle (5½ miles) and thence to Laggan (2 miles).

Cluny Castle, rebuilt in the 19th century, was the home of Cluny Macpherson, who helped to rescue Prince Charles Edward, and of other chieftains of the clan. Laggan is a small village at the beginning of the military road built by General Wade in 1745 over the Corrieyairack Pass to Fort Augustus.

A86 across the river to Drumgask ($\frac{1}{2}$ mile), then up Strath Mashie and over the watershed to Kinloch Laggan ($6\frac{1}{2}$ miles).

Drumgask is a hamlet at the foot of the strath, above which rises the precipitous wooded hill of the Black Craig, capped by a pre-historic fort. Kinloch Laggan is at the head of Loch Laggan (7 miles long), now part of a hydro-electric scheme; its delightfully wooded shores enclose fine sands when the water is low. Above the loch on the north rises the formidable bulk of Creag Meagaidh.

A86 on beside Loch Laggan to Moy Lodge (7 miles), descending thence past Loch Moy to Tulloch (6 miles).

Moy Lodge is at the foot of Loch Laggan. From here, the road goes down through the bleak upper part of Glen Spean, passing Loch Moy, a reservoir 4 miles long held in by the Laggan Dam (1934), 170 feet high and 700 feet long. Tulloch is a farmstead at the north end of the savage defile that holds Loch Treig. In the charming lower part of the glen, called the Braes of Lochaber, is the wooded gorge of Achluachrach, with its waterfalls, and to the south rise the imposing eastern peaks of the grand Ben Nevis range.

A86 on to Roybridge ($5\frac{1}{2}$ miles).

Roybridge is a small village at the foot of Glen Roy, which is famous for its ' Parallel Roads '. These are actually three pairs of terraces along the hillsides, formed by the lapping shore waters of a glacial lake that once filled the glen.

A86 on to Spean Bridge (3 miles), then A82, the outgoing route, to Fort William ($9\frac{1}{2}$ miles).

10. Glen Garry and Strath Spey, Deeside and Glen Shee

This tour starts from the popular tourist resort of Pitlochry, in a charming though partly man-made landscape, with the fine ' theatre of the Highlands '. It follows the Garry upstream through the lovely Pass of Killiecrankie and past Blair Castle, the baronial mansion of the Dukes of Atholl, then from the wild Pass of Drum-ochter descends to the beautiful Strath Spey, where the places of interest include the museum of Highland life at Kingussie and the striking new Holiday Centre at Aviemore. From the planned town of Grantown-on-Spey, the tour recrosses the Grampians by a hilly road to the delightfully wooded valley of the Dee, famous for Balmoral Castle, the Highland residence of the queen. From Brae-mar, another favoured tourist centre, the route crosses the high-lying Cairnwell Pass and descends to the long Glen Shee, now a popular way of approach for winter-sports enthusiasts.

Pitlochry is a favourite holiday resort and touring centre well situ-ated above the glen of the Tummel and surrounded by charmingly wooded hills. The landscape in the neighbourhood has been changed but not spoiled by an extensive hydro-electric scheme, which has included the creation of Loch Faskally, a new lake formed in 1947-50 by damming the river below the town. Beside the dam is a remarkable fish ladder, 900 feet long, up which some 5,000 salmon pass every year. The road on the west side, affording charming views of the wood-fringed loch and the glen, leads to Loch Tummel, greatly extended by being incorporated in the hydro-electric scheme. From it some 2,700-million gallons of water are piped each day to the Clunie Power Station, below the Linn of Tummel, once-famous falls near the junction of the Tummel with the Garry. The excellent Festival Theatre at Pitlochry, opened in 1951, has a summer season of repertory plays.

From Pitlochry by A9 along the hillside east of the Tummel and the Garry and through the Pass of Killiecrankie ($3\frac{1}{2}$ miles).

The Pass of Killiecrankie, breaching the Highland Fault, is a beautiful tree-filled gorge through which the Garry forces its way to join the Tummel. On the slopes to the north was fought the Battle of Killiecrankie (1689) in which the forces of William III were defeated by an army of Highlanders, supporting the cause of James VII and II, and led by John Graham of Claverhouse, ' Bonnie Dundee ', who was mortally wounded.

A9 on to Blair Atholl (4 miles).

Blair Atholl, the highest village in the Strath of Garry, stands at the foot of Glen Tilt and is enclosed by lovely woods. Blair Castle (admission May to mid-October, weekdays 10 to 6, Sundays 2 to 6; Sundays and Mondays only from Easter to the end of April), the seat of the Murrays, Dukes of Atholl, is an impressive baronial

N

Grantown-on-Spey

A95

Dulnain Bridge

A939

Bridge of Brown

A95

Tomintoul

A9

Aviemore

Boat of Garten

A939

Lecht Road

Alvie

Cock Bridge

Kincraig

Colnabaichin

A9

Loch Insh

Gairnshiel Lodge

Newtonmore

Kingussie

A9

Cairngorm Mountains

Invercauld Bridge

A93

Crat

Braemar

Balmor Castle

Dalwhinnie

Glen Clunie Lodge

Pass of Drumochter

Cairnwell Pass

A93

Loch Ericht

Dalnaspidal

Dalnacardoch Lodge

Devil's Elbow

A9

Glen Garry

Spittal of Glensh

Loch Garry

Calvine

Blair Atholl

Straloch

A9

A924

Glen Shee

A93

Pass of Killiecrankie

Moulin

A924

Kirkmichael

Loch Tummel

Loch Faskally

Pitlochry

B950

A93

A9

Ballinluig

Bridge of Cally

To Blairgowrie

Tour 10
159 miles

mansion of the 13th century and later, containing many Jacobite relics and interesting portraits, and notable tapestries, porcelain, and furniture. Viscount Dundee (see above) is buried in the church of Old Blair, near by.

A9 on to Calvine (5 miles), then through Glen Garry to Dalnacardoch Lodge ($6\frac{1}{2}$ miles) and on to Dalnaspidal (5 miles), and thence to the Pass of Drumochter (2 miles).

Calvine is a hamlet at the foot of the long Glen Garry, where it is joined by Glen Errochty. Beyond Dalnacardoch Lodge is Wade's Stone, marking the place where the troops making the road from Dunkeld for General Wade met those who had worked over from Inverness (1729). Dalnaspidal is in a wild situation where the road, leaving the Garry, which emerges from Loch Garry, to the south, begins the final ascent to the summit of the Pass of Drumochter (1,506 feet), crossed also by the Perth-Inverness railway, which here reaches the highest summit (1,484 feet) of any railway in Britain (except that up Snowdon).

A9 on, descending to Dalwhinnie (6 miles) and thence to Newtonmore ($10\frac{1}{2}$ miles).

Dalwhinnie is a small village in an exposed position near the north end of the desolate Loch Ericht. Newtonmore is a long village in well-wooded country near the head of Strath Spey. Clan Macpherson House (admission weekdays, Easter-September, 10 to 12 and 2 to 6) is now the interesting small museum of the clan, who held sway over this district.

A9 on through the strath to Kingussie ($3\frac{1}{2}$ miles) and thence to Kincraig ($5\frac{1}{2}$ miles).

Kingussie is a small town in the broad and beautifully wooded strath of the Spey, north of the mountainous district of Badenoch. Near the main street at the east end is the fascinating Highland Folk Museum (admission weekdays, May-September, 10 to 4), which includes an 18th century house containing textiles, domestic utensils, craft work, etc. In the grounds are an old barn, with agricultural implements, and representative buildings brought from various parts of northern Scotland. Kincraig is a village on the river below its outflow from Loch Insh. The parish church of Insh, on the opposite bank, occupies a site used for Christian worship since the 6th century.

A9 on through Strath Spey to Alvie ($3\frac{1}{2}$ miles) and thence to Aviemore ($2\frac{1}{2}$ miles).

Alvie is a hamlet on the little Loch Alvie, which is separated from the river by the wooded Tor of Alvie. Aviemore is a long, plain village on the Spey, and a popular tourist centre and winter-sports resort, the most convenient base for exploring the Cairngorm Mountains which rise to the south-east. Near the station is the successful new Holiday Centre, opened in 1966, the first of its kind in Britain, with hotels and restaurants, a theatre and concert hall, and numerous sporting facilities. Beyond the river extends the delightful Rothiemurchus Forest, which preserves many survivors of the once-extensive Caledonian Forest and encloses the charming small lake of Loch-an-Eilean.

A9 on for $4\frac{1}{2}$ miles, then A95 (right), passing north of Boat of Garten (2 miles), and on to Dulnain Bridge ($5\frac{1}{2}$ miles).

Boat of Garten, on a by-road to the right, is a village named from a former ferry across the Spey. The small Loch Garten, in Abernethy Forest beyond the river, is a nesting place of ospreys, which are carefully preserved. Dulnain Bridge is a village on a tributary of the Spey, in the richly wooded strath.

A95 on to Grantown-on-Spey (3 miles).

Grantown-on-Spey is a granite-built market town, well laid out after 1776 by Sir James Grant of Grant, with a wide main street planted with trees. It is frequented for angling and golf in summer and for ski-ing in winter. Inverallan Church, near the square, has a magnificent oak pulpit of 1639 and old panelling with shields of arms.

A939 across the Spey and thence over a ridge south-west of the Hills of Cromdale to Bridge of Brown ($9\frac{1}{2}$ miles); then across Strath Avon to Tomintoul ($4\frac{1}{2}$ miles).

Bridge of Brown is a hamlet charmingly situated on a tributary of the Avon. Tomintoul, the highest village in the Highlands (about 1,160 feet), though Wanlockhead and Leadhills in the Lowlands are higher, is a summer and angling resort and a winter-sports centre on a ridge above Strath Avon, with views of the Cairngorms to the south-west.

Most of the next section of the road, as far as Crathie, on Deeside, is hilly and narrow, with space for only a single line of cars, but there are numerous and adequate passing places. The long descent to Cock Bridge, with steep gradients and sharp bends, requires care. A939 on up the glen of the Conglass Water by the Lecht Road and over a moorland pass (2,090 feet), descending thence to Cock Bridge ($9\frac{1}{2}$ miles).

The Lecht Road, part of a military road built in 1754, crosses a north-east extension of the Grampians towards the Ladder Hills, with wide-spreading views. Cock Bridge is a hamlet on the headwaters of the Don, to the south of which is Corgarff Castle, an unusual tower-house of about 1550 (recently restored) surrounded by a wall added in the 18th century.

A939 east to Colnabaichin ($2\frac{1}{2}$ miles), then south over a range of the Grampians to Gairnshiel Lodge (6 miles), in Glen Gairn, and on over another moorland range to Crathie ($5\frac{1}{2}$ miles).

Crathie, a hamlet on the north bank of the Dee, in the beautifully wooded valley, has a granite church of 1895 that is attended by the royal family when in residence at Balmoral Castle (admission to gardens only, usually May-July, weekdays, 10 to 5), the entrance to which is beyond the river. The castle, practically hidden by its enclosing woods, is the Highland home of the sovereign and was a favourite retreat of Queen Victoria. It is a mansion in the Scottish baronial style (1856), designed by William Smith of Aberdeen with the assistance of Prince Albert, who had bought the estate and who also planted the grounds with rare conifers and other trees. On the hills to the south are commemorative cairns to members of Queen Victoria's family. A brief view of the castle is obtained from the Braemar road 1 mile west of Crathie.

A93 up the valley of the Dee to Invercauld Bridge ($3\frac{1}{2}$ miles).

Invercauld Bridge. Here, where the river is crossed, among delightful woods, near the Old Bridge of Dee (1752), is the entrance to the enlarged 15th century Invercauld House, the seat of the Farquharson family. The Earl of Mar sent out his address from here, calling for the support of the clans in the first Jacobite rising, and here the chiefs assembled (1715). Braemar Castle (admission daily, May-October, 10 to 6) is a tall Scottish baronial house built in 1628 by the Erskines, Earls of Mar, and restored and sold to the Farquharsons in the 18th century.

A93 on, passing Braemar Castle, to Braemar ($5\frac{1}{2}$ miles).

Braemar is a pleasant small town and a popular summer and winter resort on the Clunie Water, a tributary of the Dee, surrounded by charming mountain scenery. The Invercauld Arms Hotel stands on the site of the mound where the Earl of Mar raised his standard in 1715. Near by are the Invercauld Studios Theatre, in a converted church, and the Invercauld Galleries, where an exhibition of Scottish handicrafts is held in summer. R. L. Stevenson wrote much of *Treasure Island* in 1881 at a cottage nearly opposite. The Braemar Gathering, a colourful occasion in September, with Highland games, etc., is usually patronised by royalty.

A93 up the valley of the Clunie Water to Glen Clunie Lodge ($5\frac{1}{2}$ miles), ascending thence to the Cairnwell Pass (4 miles).

Glen Clunie affords a fine retrospect of Ben Avon, one of the Cairngorm mountains. The Cairnwell Pass (2,199 feet), between The Cairnwell, on the west, and the great bulk of Glas Maol, is the highest pass on a main road in Britain and a favourite base for winter-sports.

A93 on, descending to the steep zigzag known as the Devil's Elbow ($\frac{1}{2}$ mile), not really difficult, but care is required on wet or icy conditions, and thence down Glen Beg or Beag to Spittal of Glenshee (5 miles).

Spittal of Glenshee is a hamlet and winter-sports resort finely placed at the foot of bare and narrow Glen Beg and its junction with the wild Glen Lochsie, which comes in on the west from one of the loneliest regions of the Grampians, the two glens forming Glen Shee.

A93 on down the rugged Glen Shee for 8 miles, then B950 (right), crossing a ridge to Kirkmichael (3½ miles). [A93 goes on through Glen Shee to Bridge of Cally (5 miles), at the junction of the glen with Strathardle and thence to Blairgowrie (see Tour 3, page 22).]

Kirkmichael is a pleasant village on the Ardle, in the charmingly wooded Strathardle, surrounded by fine open moorlands.

A924 (right) through Strathardle to Straloch (4 miles) and thence up Glen Brerachan to a moorland saddle (3½ miles), descending thence to Moulin (5 miles), a hamlet on the hillside above Pitlochry (1 mile).

Straloch is a hamlet at the junction of Glen Brerachan with Glen Fearnach to form Strathardle. From the road summit (1,260 feet) a wonderful panorama opens over a great expanse of the Central Highlands, extending from Ben Lawers and Schichallion in the south-west to Beinn a' Ghlo in the north.

Index of Places